HOW GOD GROWS
A GIRL of
WISDOM

A DEVOTIONAL

HOW GOD GROWS
A GIRL of
WISDOM

A DEVOTIONAL

JoAnne Simmons

BARBOUR **kidz**
A Division of Barbour Publishing

Published by Barbour Publishing, Inc., 1810 Barbour Drive, Uhrichsville, Ohio 44683, www.barbourbooks.com

Our mission is to inspire the world with the life-changing message of the Bible.

Printed in the United States of America.

000845 0721 SP

INTRODUCTION

Hi! I'm JoAnne Simmons, and my daughters are Jodi and Lilly. Our first two books together were *How God Grows a Girl of Grace* and *How God Grows a Praying Girl*, and now we're writing even more encouragement to share, hoping to help you learn more about how to be a wise girl! Maybe you instantly think of an owl when you hear the word *wise*. That's a common and cute symbol of wisdom. But in this book, we'll talk about how real wisdom comes from the one true God who is the Creator of owls, the Creator of you—and the Creator of everything else too! His Word promises that He loves to give wisdom to those who ask—and not just a little wisdom but a lot! He loves you very much and wants you to make the best and wisest choices in your life. So read on, and as you do, please know that we are praying for you to be a girl who loves to grow in God's wisdom, just as we pray that for ourselves.

THE BEGINNING OF WISDOM

*The works of His hands are faithful and right. All His Laws
are true. They stand strong forever and ever. They are done
by what is true and right. . . . The fear of the Lord is the
beginning of wisdom. All who obey His Laws have good
understanding. His praise lasts forever.*
PSALM 111:7–8, 10

So what is wisdom, exactly? . . . Is it just being smart and reading lots of books? Is it what you get once you've lived so long that you're old and wrinkly? Well, you can gain knowledge by reading lots of books and living a long time, for sure; but wisdom comes from the one true God, who teaches us how to apply the knowledge we gain over the years. Wisdom basically means being able to figure out right from wrong and having good sense or good judgment. That might not sound popular and cool, but God's wisdom really is awesome! Having it and using it makes for the best kind of life. And the Bible tells us that the fear of God—meaning having faith in and respect for God—is the beginning of wisdom. So, do you want to have wisdom, and do you have faith in and respect for God? Then keep on reading!

*Dear God, I've never thought much about having wisdom.
Could You please help me grow in this area and teach
me what You want me to know? Thank You! Amen.*

JESUS IS THE ONLY WAY

*Jesus told him, "I am the way, the truth,
and the life. No one can come to the
Father except through me."*
JOHN 14:6 NLT

To have true faith in and respect for God (which then leads to gaining wisdom) means that you will want to have a relationship with Jesus Christ as your Savior. Jesus is God in human form who came to earth as a baby to grow up and live and love and show all people the way to have a relationship with God in heaven forever. Then Jesus died on the cross to save people from the bad things they do, their sin. Three days later He rose again to prove that He could conquer death and offer eternal life to all who believe in Him alone as their Savior from sin. If you have never prayed to ask Jesus to be your Savior, then pray something like this:

....

*Dear Jesus, I believe in You as God and Savior!
You died on the cross to save me from my sins,
and You didn't stay dead. You rose again!
And because that's true, I trust that You will
give me eternal life too. Please help me to
live my life following Your ways and growing
in Your love and wisdom. Amen.*

ASK GOD FOR IT

If you do not have wisdom, ask God for it. He is
always ready to give it to you and will never say you
are wrong for asking. You must have faith as you ask
Him. You must not doubt. Anyone who doubts is
like a wave which is pushed around by the sea.
JAMES 1:5–6

Once you have accepted Jesus as your Savior and have begun a new life of faith in the one true God, then you can begin to ask God for His wisdom. God loves you and is interested in every single thing about you. In everything you do and think and say throughout your days—in your home with your family, at school with classmates and teachers, in your activities with friends, and even when you're just hanging out by yourself— God wants to help you. He wants you to ask for and apply His wisdom as you make choices and learn and grow. Don't ever doubt it. God doesn't want you to be like a wave that's pushed around by the sea. No, if you constantly use His wisdom in your life, you will be strong and stable, ready and able to do the good things God planned for you when He created you.

Dear God, please give me lots and lots and lots of wisdom
for everything in my life. Help me to trust You and use
that wisdom exactly the way You want me to. Amen.

YOUR HELPER,
THE HOLY SPIRIT

*The Helper is the Holy Spirit. The Father will send
Him in My place. He will teach you everything and
help you remember everything I have told you.*
JOHN 14:26

Jesus promised His followers that after He died and rose again and went to heaven, He would not leave them alone. He would send the very best Helper—God's Holy Spirit who comes to live in each person who asks Jesus to be their Savior. So if you have asked Jesus to be your Savior, then you have the Holy Spirit in you too. When you ask God for wisdom, you can remember that He is right there inside you, ready to give wisdom to you right away and help you know what to do and think and say in any kind of situation.

*Dear God, thank You for Your Holy Spirit
living in me. Help me to learn and grow in
all the things You want me to know. Amen.*

TREASURE TROVE,
PART 1

*All the Holy Writings are God-given and are made alive
by Him. Man is helped when he is taught God's Word.
It shows what is wrong. It changes the way of a man's life.
It shows him how to be right with God. It gives the man who
belongs to God everything he needs to work well for Him.*
2 TIMOTHY 3:16–17

God can communicate with us in any way He chooses. He shows us He is real by His amazing creation all around us. He proves Himself faithful to us when we talk to Him and He answers our prayers. He shows us His love in infinite ways and through the many people who take care of us and encourage us and bless us. And He speaks to us in written words, especially through the Bible. When we choose to believe it as God's main way of teaching and guiding us, and then read it, follow it, and put it into action in our lives, it is an absolute treasure trove of the wisdom we need.

*Dear God, please help me to love Your Word and
all the wisdom You give to me in it. Help me want to
read it every day and learn more about You and how
You want to guide me in the best kind of life. Amen.*

TReasure TROVe, Part 2

*God's Word is living and powerful. It is sharper
than a sword that cuts both ways. It cuts straight
into where the soul and spirit meet and it divides them.
It cuts into the joints and bones. It tells what the heart
is thinking about and what it wants to do. No one can
hide from God. His eyes see everything we do. We must
give an answer to God for what we have done.*
HEBREWS 4:12–13

God's Word, which is full of wisdom for us, is not just some ancient book that should gather dust on a shelf. It is alive and powerful as we read it, and God uses it to speak to us. More scriptures that show us how powerful and important God's Word should be to us are these:

- "Everything that was written in the Holy Writings long ago was written to teach us. By not giving up, God's Word gives us strength and hope" (Romans 15:4).

- "How sweet is Your Word to my taste! It is sweeter than honey to my mouth! I get understanding from Your Law and so I hate every false way. Your Word is a lamp to my feet and a light to my path" (Psalm 119:103–105).

*Dear God, please speak directly to me through
Your Word every day. Guide me and help
me to listen and obey well. Amen.*

TREASURE TROVE, PART 3

The grass dries up. The flower loses its color.
But the Word of our God stands forever.
ISAIAH 40:8

Since the Bible is our main source of wisdom given to us by God, we should make reading it a regular part of our daily lives. We shouldn't just flip through it here and there. We shouldn't just carry it to church and not touch it the rest of the week. If you spend time in it regularly, you will learn more and more about God and His people and how He wants His Word to guide you in your life today. The Bible has sixty-six books in all, and they are separated into the Old and New Testaments. Throughout this devotional, we'll talk a little about each of the books to help you understand the purpose of each one and grow in your knowledge of the Bible so that you might want to learn more from it to grow in wisdom and faith and relationship with God for your whole life!

Dear God, please help me to love Your Word and spend time reading and studying it regularly. I want to grow in wisdom and grow closer to You! Amen.

WISDOM FROM THE BOOK OF GENESIS

In the beginning God made from
nothing the heavens and the earth.
GENESIS 1:1

The word *genesis* means "beginnings." That's fitting for the title of the very first book of the Bible! In this book, written by Moses, we learn about the beginning of our earth and how God created it. We learn about the very first people, Adam and Eve. We also learn how sin began when Adam and Eve chose to disobey God. We learn about Noah and the ark. (That's our favorite story in Genesis! We love animals!) And we learn about the beginning of God's special family of people, the Israelites, through whom He would send His Son, Jesus Christ, to offer salvation to all people. You can learn much from the book of Genesis if you take time to study it.

Dear God, thank You for the book of Genesis. Help me
as I read it and keep coming back to it in the future.
Teach me what You want me to learn from it to apply
to my life and to share with others. Amen.

WHAT LOVE IS

*We have come to know and believe the love God
has for us. God is love. If you live in love, you live
by the help of God and God lives in you.*
1 JOHN 4:16

⤳

What are your first thoughts when you think of love? When we think of it, we think of love for each other in our family, love for our friends, and love for our two silly dogs, Jasper and Daisy. We care about each other and want to help each other, no matter what, even if we get mad at each other sometimes. We bring joy and laughter to each other as we spend time together. The reason we know anything at all about love is because God is love and He showed us His love through His Son Jesus, who loves us so much that He died to save us. People have a lot of mixed-up ideas about what love is, and so we constantly need to ask God to give us *His* wisdom about love and how best to share love with others.

....

*Dear God, You are love and You show love better
than anyone else. Please give me Your perfect
wisdom about knowing real love and sharing real
love in the best and healthiest ways—Your ways—
my whole life. Thank You! Amen.*

OBEY AND HONOR

Invest in truth and wisdom, discipline and good sense,
and don't part with them. Make your father truly
happy by living right and showing sound judgment.
Make your parents proud, especially your mother.
PROVERBS 23:23–25 CEV

Maybe sometimes you get a little tired of being reminded by your parents that you need to obey. But it's not just parents who tell their kids to obey. *God* is the One who put that rule in place first. It's one of the Ten Commandments. Exodus 20:12 says, "Honor your father and your mother, so your life may be long in the land the Lord your God gives you." And Ephesians 6:1–3 says, "Children, as Christians, obey your parents. This is the right thing to do. Respect your father and mother. This is the first Law given that had a promise. The promise is this: If you respect your father and mother, you will live a long time and your life will be full of many good things."

It might not always feel fun, but obeying and honoring your parents is the right and wise thing to do. Don't forget that we parents must obey too—we should always be obeying God, our heavenly Father.

Dear God, please help me not to disobey my parents.
Help me to have a good attitude and remember that
You have called me to honor and obey my parents and
most importantly to honor and obey You! Amen.

WISDOM FROM THE
BOOK OF EXODUS

*God saw the people of Israel
and He cared about them.*
EXODUS 2:25

The word *exodus* means "departure," and the main purpose of the book of Exodus, written by Moses, is to share how God rescued His people, the Israelites, out of slavery in Egypt. You've probably heard some of the stories in Exodus of the plagues on Egypt and how God parted the Red Sea (amazing!) for His people to safely walk through when the Egyptians were chasing them down. Exodus is when we first learn of the Ten Commandments too. Do you know all of them? If not, look them up in Exodus 20:3–17. And don't stop there. You can learn much from the book of Exodus if you take time to study it.

*Dear God, thank You for the book of Exodus. Help me
as I read it and keep coming back to it in the future.
Teach me what You want me to learn from it to apply
to my life and to share with others. Amen.*

WISDOM FOR SIBLINGS

*Pray and give thanks for those who make trouble for you.
Yes, pray for them instead of talking against them. Be happy
with those who are happy. Be sad with those who are sad.
Live in peace with each other. Do not act or think with pride.
Be happy to be with poor people. Keep yourself from thinking
you are so wise. When someone does something bad to you,
do not pay him back with something bad.*
ROMANS 12:14–17

"It was the best of times; it was the worst of times" is the
famous opening line from a famous old book called *A Tale of
Two Cities* by Charles Dickens. It makes us think of times with
siblings because they sure can have the best of times and worst
of times together, right? Jodi and Lilly know all about that.
And so do I, from growing up with three siblings. Sometimes
brothers and sisters need to ask for a double, or even triple,
dose of God's wisdom in the worst of times. This scripture
in Romans 12 can help in a huge way. If siblings read it and
apply it, they will greatly improve their relationships and have
far more "best of times" than "worst of times."

*Dear God, please help me to have mostly good times
with my siblings. Please help us to follow the wisdom in
Your Word to have great relationships together. Amen.*

Love and Forgive

Peter came to Jesus and said, "Lord, how many times may my brother sin against me and I forgive him, up to seven times?" Jesus said to him, "I tell you, not seven times but seventy times seven!"
MATTHEW 18:21–22

Sometimes the people you love the most are the ones who can drive you crazy the most, right? We get it. We spend more time with the people we love most, and that means there is more opportunity to annoy each other and fight. But there's also more opportunity to love and forgive each other too. And the Bible says that because God loves and forgives us so much, we should do the same and forgive others bunches too—seventy times seven as much! That's a math problem that means however much you first think you might need to forgive, you need to go way above and beyond that amount—because God goes way above and beyond at loving and forgiving you. We need His wisdom to know how to love well and forgive well too.

Dear God, please help me to do my best at forgiving others in above-and-beyond kinds of ways like You forgive me. Amen.

WISDOM FROM THE BOOK OF LEVITICUS

The Lord said to Moses, "Say to all the people of Israel, 'Be holy, for I the Lord your God am holy.'"
LEVITICUS 19:1–2

~~~

The book of Leviticus gives detailed instructions about how God wanted the Israelites to live and to worship Him. Our one true God alone is holy and worthy of all devotion and praise! We hope you love to sing to Him like we do! The instructions in Leviticus also included sacrifices that the Israelites should make to God, but one day all those sacrifices would be replaced by God's Son, Jesus Christ, making the ultimate sacrifice by giving His life on the cross to pay for the sin of all people forever. You can learn much from the book of Leviticus if you take time to study it.

Dear God, thank You for the book of Leviticus. Help me as I read it and keep coming back to it in the future. Teach me what You want me to learn from it to apply to my life and to share with others. Amen.

BE HONEST ABOUT EVERYTHING

*The Lord hates lying lips, but those
who speak the truth are His joy.*
PROVERBS 12:22

Since God hates lying lips, then so should we! And that means we should be honest about everything—big things and little things. If we are, then we become trustworthy people. Bosses and leaders and teachers notice consistent honesty, and good ones usually want to reward us and give new opportunities because of it. Luke 16:10–12 says, "He that is faithful with little things is faithful with big things also. He that is not honest with little things is not honest with big things. If you have not been faithful with riches of this world, who will trust you with true riches? If you have not been faithful in that which belongs to another person, who will give you things to have as your own?"

*Dear God, please help me never to lie, even about
little things. I want to be wise and honest
and trustworthy in all things. Amen.*

MORE ABOUT THE TRUTH

*As Jesus said these things, many people put their trust
in Him. He said to the Jews who believed, "If you keep
and obey My Word, then you are My followers for sure.
You will know the truth and the truth will make you free."*
JOHN 8:30–32

～～～

Honesty and truth are so super important, especially in a world
where they often seem harder and harder to find. Let God and
the Bible be your number one source of truth, and let all of
these scriptures grow you in wisdom about how important it is!

- "The honor of good people will lead them, but those who
  hurt others will be destroyed by their own false ways"
  (Proverbs 11:3).

- "A man who tells lies about someone will be punished.
  He who tells lies will be lost" (Proverbs 19:9).

- "Show me Your ways, O Lord. Teach me Your paths. Lead
  me in Your truth and teach me. For You are the God Who
  saves me" (Psalm 25:4–5).

- "Do your best to know that God is pleased with you. Be
  as a workman who has nothing to be ashamed of. Teach
  the words of truth in the right way. Do not listen to
  foolish talk about things that mean nothing. It only leads
  people farther away from God" (2 Timothy 2:15–16).

*Dear God, You and Your Word are the ultimate truth! Help me
to love You and the Bible more and more each day. Amen.*

WISDOM WHEN YOU'RE WORRIED, PART 1

*Give all your worries to Him
because He cares for you.*
1 PETER 5:7

The best and wisest thing you can do when you're feeling worried is remember that God wants to take those worries away from you. His Word says to give them all to Him. Not just the big and worst worries—but *all* of them. Now, if you're worried about your upcoming test at school, does that mean you should give the worry about it to God and then just skip studying? Of course not. Let the worry motivate you to do the good work of studying, but then give the worry over to God. If you know you've studied and prepared well, then you have no need to worry. Just go and take your test, trusting that God will help you recall the things you learned as you studied, and He will help you do your best.

*Dear God, thank You that You care about my worries.
Please let them motivate me to do the good things I need
to while I give the stressful part of the worry over to You.
Please replace it with Your peace. Thank You! Amen.*

WISDOM WHEN YOU'RE WORRIED, PART 2

"Do not worry about your life. Do not worry about what you are going to eat and drink. Do not worry about what you are going to wear. Is not life more important than food? Is not the body more important than clothes? Look at the birds in the sky. They do not plant seeds. They do not gather grain. They do not put grain into a building to keep. Yet your Father in heaven feeds them! Are you not more important than the birds?"
MATTHEW 6:25–26

Maybe it's not a test you're worried about these days. Maybe it's much worse. Maybe you're worried about having enough money, food, and clothes because of a hard situation in your family. If that's the case, this scripture in Matthew can give you great peace. Read it over and over until it's stuck in your brain, so that you never forget that God takes care of you. No matter what happens in your life, He knows what you need and will provide for you.

....

Dear God, thank You for showing me how much I matter to You! Please give me the wisdom to remember that I never need to worry because You will always take care of me. Amen.

WISDOM WHEN YOU'RE WORRIED, PART 3

*"For God so loved the world that He gave His only Son.
Whoever puts his trust in God's Son will not be
lost but will have life that lasts forever."*
JOHN 3:16

⟿

Maybe you're worried about sickness and death for a family member or friend, or even for yourself. And the hard truth is that every single one of us will die someday. That's why knowing Jesus as Savior is *so* important. Only He can promise us eternal life, because only He rose to life again after dying for our sin. While death is so sad here on earth for those who are left behind to miss their loved one, Jesus gives hope. There is great joy and peace in trusting that every person who believes in Him as the one and only Savior will be in heaven forever in a perfect new body that will never, ever die again.

*Dear God, thank You for the hope of heaven for all who trust
in You. Please help me to share about You with others so more
people know You as Savior and will have eternal life. Amen.*

WISDOM FROM THE BOOK OF NUMBERS

"If the Lord is pleased with us, then He will bring us into this land and give it to us. It is a land which flows with milk and honey. Only do not go against the Lord."
NUMBERS 14:8–9

The book of Numbers starts out with God telling Moses to take a census, which means a counting, of all the men ages twenty and older of the nation of Israel. The total number was 603,550! The book goes on to describe how the people of Israel wandered in the wilderness after God delivered them from slavery in Egypt. They could have reached the land God had promised to give them in just two weeks, but because they had little faith in God and were very ungrateful and whiny, God punished them. Much can be learned from the book of Numbers, especially about being grateful and having great faith in God, no matter what. He loves and wants to bless people, but He will punish people who rebel and complain and don't trust Him.

Dear God, thank You for the book of Numbers. Help me as I read it and keep coming back to it in the future. Teach me what You want me to learn from it to apply to my life and to share with others. Amen.

BE HUMBLE, NOT PROUD

Let yourself be brought low before the Lord.
Then He will lift you up and help you.
JAMES 4:10

What is the story of your most embarrassing moment? Does it still make you cringe or turn red? It might make you feel so silly, but do you know that it's wise to be able to laugh at yourself? When you can laugh at yourself, it helps show that you are humble. Being humble is the opposite of being proud and thinking too highly of yourself. It's good to be confident and have good self-esteem, but it's not good to take that so far that you think you are better than others or can never make a mistake or that you have no need for God in your life. Being humble means that you know you mess up sometimes and need forgiveness and grace from God and from others. And being humble means that you know there are always ways you can learn and grow.

....

Dear God, please give me wisdom about
knowing the difference between being proud
and being humble. Help me to be humble and
always know my need for Your grace and love!

PraY ABOUT EVerYTHING

Do not worry. Learn to pray about everything.
Give thanks to God as you ask Him for what you
need. The peace of God is much greater than the
human mind can understand. This peace will keep
your hearts and minds through Christ Jesus.

PHILIPPIANS 4:6–7

Instead of worrying, God wants you to pray about everything. As you pray and ask God for what you need, don't forget to focus on your blessings. List them in your head or out loud, or write them down on paper and thank God for them. (Maybe you have a fun, fuzzy-covered journal to write in like Jodi and Lilly do!) When you see the many ways God has already blessed you and provided for you, it helps you remember that you don't need to worry. He will always continue to bless you and provide for you. Thank Him and praise Him for who He is and all He has done as you pray, and let His amazing peace fill you up and chase away whatever worries you might have.

....

Dear God, thank You for everything!
Please chase away every worry and fill
me with Your incredible peace. Amen.

WHY PRAY?

*Come close to God and
He will come close to you.*
JAMES 4:8

Sometimes you might wonder why praying matters, especially when the Bible says God already knows everything you're going to say before you even say it (Psalm 139:4; Matthew 6:8). But maybe you have a best friend who can almost seem to read your mind that way too. If she knows you so well, then why do you care about spending time with her? Because you love her and have so much fun being together and doing things together, right? That's the way God wants to be your absolute best, best Friend. He loves you and knows you more than any person ever possibly could, and He hopes you will simply want to spend time with Him and be included in the good things He is doing.

*Dear God, I want to be close to You through prayer and
through reading Your Word. Help me to look forward to
spending time with You as my very best Friend of all. Amen.*

WISDOM FROM THE BOOK OF DEUTERONOMY

"Love the Lord your God with all your heart and with all your soul and with all your strength. Keep these words in your heart that I am telling you today. Do your best to teach them to your children. Talk about them when you sit in your house and when you walk on the road and when you lie down and when you get up."

DEUTERONOMY 6:5–7

Moses wrote the book of Deuteronomy to remind the people of Israel about all God had done for them and provided for them and taught them. Moses reminded the people again about the Ten Commandments too. God also wants you to remember regularly all He has done for you and provided for you and taught you. He doesn't want you to forget the good instructions He has given through His Word to obey Him and live the life He has created you for. He loves and disciplines and forgives and wants to bless His people, and that includes you!

....

Dear God, thank You for the book of Deuteronomy. Help me as I read it and keep coming back to it in the future. Teach me what You want me to learn from it to apply to my life and to share with others. Amen.

BUSY IS NOT BETTER, Part 1

As they went on their way, they came to a town where a woman named Martha lived. She cared for Jesus in her home. Martha had a sister named Mary. Mary sat at the feet of Jesus and listened to all He said. Martha was working hard getting the supper ready. She came to Jesus and said, "Do You see that my sister is not helping me? Tell her to help me." Jesus said to her, "Martha, Martha, you are worried and troubled about many things. Only a few things are important, even just one. Mary has chosen the good thing. It will not be taken away from her."
LUKE 10:38–42

How cool to think of having Jesus over for supper, right? Martha and Mary got to experience that, and their story can help us to be wise with how we spend our time. Martha was keeping very busy doing good things to make a nice meal and take care of Jesus. But she was upset that her sister, Mary, wasn't helping enough. Can you relate? Do you ever feel like you're the one doing all the work when others are supposed to be helping you? It's frustrating, for sure! But in this case, Jesus gently told Martha that Mary was doing the very best thing—listening to His teaching.

Dear God, please remind me that keeping busy doing things is never more important than listening to what You want to teach me. Amen.

BUSY IS NOT BETTER, PART 2

*Obey the Word of God. If you hear only and do not act,
you are only fooling yourself. Anyone who hears the Word
of God and does not obey is like a man looking at his face
in a mirror. After he sees himself and goes away, he forgets
what he looks like. But the one who keeps looking into God's
perfect Law and does not forget it will do what it says and
be happy as he does it. God's Word makes men free.*

JAMES 1:22–25

We could take that story of Martha and Mary too far and use it as an excuse for laziness, saying things like, "Well, I guess Jesus said I don't ever need to clean my room. I'll just lie in my bed forever, reading my Bible." But that's not right! God created you to do good things, and that requires getting out of bed! With wisdom, we can understand there's a balance between hearing God's Word and *doing* what it says, and that balance can only happen if we put listening to and following Jesus at the top of our to-do list. Everything else we need to do should come after that number one priority!

*Dear God, please help me always to find the
right balance of listening to and following Your Word,
plus doing the good things You have created me for. Amen.*

WISDOM FROM THE BOOK OF JOSHUA

*"This book of the Law must not leave your mouth.
Think about it day and night, so you may be careful to
do all that is written in it. Then all will go well with you.
You will receive many good things. Have I not told you?
Be strong and have strength of heart! Do not be afraid or
lose faith. For the Lord your God is with you anywhere you go."*
JOSHUA 1:8–9

The book of Joshua picks up where the book of Deuteronomy ended. Moses has died and Joshua is the new leader of the nation of Israel. He's ready to lead God's people into Canaan, the promised land. The first half of Joshua tells how the Israelites defeat any armies that stand in their way as they take over Canaan. The second half tells how the Israelites divided the land among their twelve tribes. One of our favorite stories in this book is of Rahab, a brave woman who helped God's people, and God protected her and her whole family because of her great faith and courage (Joshua 2; Hebrews 11:31; James 2:25).

*Dear God, thank You for the book of Joshua.
Help me as I read it and keep coming back to it in
the future. Teach me what You want me to learn from
it to apply to my life and to share with others. Amen.*

WISDOM FOR FRIENDSHIP

Don't fool yourselves.
Bad friends will destroy you.
1 CORINTHIANS 15:33 CEV

Think about your favorite friends and why you love hanging out with them. We all need good friends in our lives, and we need to be good friends to others. But this verse makes it clear that we need a lot of wisdom about friendship too. If bad friends will destroy us, then we sure need to know how to figure out if a friend is a good friend or a bad friend. Your very best Friend is Jesus as your Savior. The best kind of friends are those who love and follow Him too and try to be as much like Him as possible. A bad friend will want to lead you into trouble and away from following Jesus. Your whole life, you will need lots of wisdom and help from God to find good friends who care about you and also to avoid bad friends who will destroy you. Never stop asking God to show you every friend's true character and which friendships to keep and which ones to walk away from.

Dear God, thank You for the gift of good friends,
and please give me lots and lots of wisdom about
friendship now and in the future. Amen.

KING SOLOMON'S REQUEST, PART 1

Now Solomon loved the Lord.
He walked in the Laws of his father David.
1 KINGS 3:3

~~~

King Solomon loved God and wanted to follow His ways, and so God wanted to bless him. First Kings 3:5 says, "The Lord came to Solomon in a special dream in Gibeon during the night. God said, 'Ask what you wish Me to give you.' " Solomon could have asked God for *anything* at all, but this is what he asked for: "Now, O Lord my God, You have made Your servant king in place of my father David. But I am only a little child. I do not know how to start or finish. Your servant is among Your people which You have chosen. They are many people. There are too many people to number. So give Your servant an understanding heart to judge Your people and know the difference between good and bad" (1 Kings 3:7–9). Wow, what a good and honorable choice! We should want to be like Solomon, recognizing that wisdom from God to know the difference between right and wrong is far more valuable than any treasure.

. . . .

Dear God, please help me to learn from
King Solomon's example and want wisdom
from You more than earthly treasure. Amen.

KING SOLOMON'S REQUEST, PART 2

*It pleased the Lord that
Solomon had asked this.*
1 KINGS 3:10

Because Solomon had chosen so well, God wanted to bless him *even more*. He said to Solomon, "You have asked this, and have not asked for a long life for yourself. You have not asked for riches, or for the life of those who hate you. But you have asked for understanding to know what is right. Because you have asked this, I have done what you said. See, I have given you a wise and understanding heart. No one has been like you before, and there will be no one like you in the future. I give you what you have not asked, also. I give you both riches and honor. So there will be no king like you all your days. And if you walk in My ways and keep My Laws and Word as your father David did, I will allow you to live a long time" (1 Kings 3:11–14).

When we choose to ask God for wisdom rather than riches, we please Him, just like Solomon did. He is our good heavenly Father who loves to bless us for choosing what's best.

. . . .

*Dear God, I trust that You love to bless me when I choose wisely.
Lots of things seem good, but please help me to choose what's
best in life. I want to please and honor You! Amen.*

Happiness or Joy?
Part 1

You will show me the way of life. Being with You is to be full of joy. In Your right hand there is happiness forever.
PSALM 16:11

Whatever makes you happy! That's a phrase you might hear a lot these days, but one we all need to be careful with—because if it's our constant goal just to be happy, we can truly ruin our lives. I'd probably be happy with a big plate of brownies to eat every single night, but that's sure not wise or good for me. I'd also really be happy if I got to go to the beach and Disney World every single week, but that's sure not wise or good for me either. Dessert and vacation can make us all really happy, but they have to be balanced wisely with healthy foods and times of work and learning. That's why joy is so much more important than happiness. Real joy is based on our relationship with Jesus and our hope of perfect heaven with Him forever, while happiness is usually just based on the situation we're in. When we focus on real joy and apply it to everything we do, that's when we can also find happiness in pretty much anything!

....

Dear God, please give me wisdom and keep me learning about how real joy in You is far better than just happiness. Amen.

Happiness or Joy?
Part 2

"The joy of the Lord is your strength."
NEHEMIAH 8:10

We need to remember how quickly and easily our feelings change. Something that made you happy last year or even a month ago might seem totally boring to you now. That's another example of how real joy is so much better than happiness. Let these scriptures help teach and guide you all of your life with wisdom about knowing real joy:

- "I will give honor and thanks to the Lord, Who has told me what to do. Yes, even at night my mind teaches me. I have placed the Lord always in front of me. Because He is at my right hand, I will not be moved. And so my heart is glad. My soul is full of joy" (Psalm 16:7–9).

- "You have never seen Him but you love Him. You cannot see Him now but you are putting your trust in Him. And you have joy so great that words cannot tell about it. You will get what your faith is looking for, which is to be saved from the punishment of sin" (1 Peter 1:8–9).

Dear God, no matter what situation I'm in or what my emotions feel like, help me to remember that my true joy is always in You.

No Secrets, Part 1

O Lord, You have looked through me and have known me.
You know when I sit down and when I get up. You understand
my thoughts from far away. You look over my path and my lying
down. You know all my ways very well. Even before I speak a
word, O Lord, You know it all. You have closed me in from behind
and in front. And You have laid Your hand upon me. All You know
is too great for me. It is too much for me to understand.
PSALM 139:1–6

You can gain wisdom from understanding that you can never keep a secret from God. Not ever. He knows absolutely everything. Even before you say a word, God knows you're going to say it. He knows every single one of your thoughts and always knows exactly what you're doing and where and when. To some people that might seem creepy, but for those who love God and want a good relationship with Him through Jesus, it never has to be. God loves you! And because He sees and knows everything about you, you should feel greatly loved and protected and cared for.

Dear God, thank You for loving me so much that
You know absolutely everything about me! Amen.

NO Secrets,
Part 2

The eyes of the Lord are in every place,
watching the bad and the good.
PROVERBS 15:3

Sometimes we might think we can hide doing the things we know are wrong, but it's just not true. In those times, we need to remember that we can keep no secrets from God. Remembering that truth can help us not to sin. God is going to see our sin, and there will be consequences. Thankfully, God loves to forgive us, like 1 John 1:9 says: "If we tell Him our sins, He is faithful and we can depend on Him to forgive us of our sins. He will make our lives clean from all sin."

Dear God, especially when I am tempted to sin
and try to hide it from You, remind me that nothing
is a secret from You. Help me to love that You are
always watching me because You care about me and
You want to keep me out of trouble. Thank You! Amen.

HELPING YOUR FRIENDS

Just as iron sharpens iron,
friends sharpen the minds of each other.
PROVERBS 27:17 CEV

Think of some ways you and your friends help each other. Maybe you're a pro at math but a friend gets easily confused by it, so you try to help her understand it. Maybe you feel like you stink at writing essays but you have a friend who is an awesome writer, and she gives you pointers to improve. Kindness and help among friends are wonderful! And they also require wisdom—because what if your friend suddenly asked you to do all of her math homework for her? That would no longer be helping but would actually hurt her. It's okay if she needs *some* help, but it's not okay for her to expect someone else to do her own work for her. And you should never expect that either. As you share kindness with your friends, always keep asking God to give you wisdom about when to step in and when to step back when they need to do things on their own to learn and grow.

....

Dear God, please give me wisdom to know when to step in and
help a friend and when to step back and be a bigger help by
letting her do things on her own to learn and grow. Amen.

WISDOM FROM THE BOOK OF JUDGES

*Then the people of Israel
sinned in the eyes of the Lord.*
JUDGES 2:11

~~~

The book of Judges tells the stories of thirteen judges who led the nation of Israel over about three hundred fifty years, including the only female judge of Israel, Deborah. You've probably heard of the strongman Samson, who was one of the judges. And Gideon is also one of the most well-known. Judges contains a lot of rough and violent stories showing how when God's people didn't care about following Him, they suffered greatly for it. But when they cried out to God, He delivered them. When we read Judges, we should be reminded to want to follow God's ways always. And we can remember that through all kinds of ups and downs, good choices and bad, blessing and suffering, God still dearly loves and never abandons His people.

*Dear God, thank You for the book of Judges.
Help me as I read it and keep coming back to it
in the future. Teach me what You want me to learn
from it to apply to my life and to share with others. Amen.*

WISDOM WHEN
YOU GET PUNISHED

*There is no joy while we are being punished. It is hard
to take, but later we can see that good came from it.*
HEBREWS 12:11

What happened the last time you got in trouble? Did you instantly think of your punishment as something to be grateful for? Probably not. We get it. That's never been our instant reaction either. But actually, if you use God's wisdom during punishment, you can choose to see the good in it. Your parents and other grown-ups in your life are truly helping you when they punish or discipline you in wise ways for things you've done wrong. They're trying to teach you never to do the same bad thing again. They're trying to teach you things like safety and honesty and respect and responsibility. Ask God to help you appreciate punishment and discipline, even if they feel awful at first. Choose to learn from them, and ask God to show you how He is maturing and teaching you because of them.

*Dear God, please give me wisdom when I've done something
wrong and then I have to face the consequences. Even though
I don't enjoy it, help me to see the good in wise punishment
and discipline, both now and in the future. Amen.*

SERVING JESUS HIMSELF

" 'Lord, when did we see You hungry and feed You?
When did we see You thirsty and give You a drink? When
did we see You a stranger and give You a room? When
did we see You had no clothes and we gave You clothes?
And when did we see You sick or in prison and we came
to You?' Then the King will say, '. . .because you did it to
one of the least of My brothers, you have done it to Me.' "
MATTHEW 25:37–40

⚜

Sometimes I feel frustrated that I can't sit down with Jesus in person. Those who lived when Jesus did were so blessed to get to know Him and His love and learn His wisdom face-to-face. But we have God's Word and the Holy Spirit, and those are incredible gifts to us! We also have the instruction on how to be extra close and serve Jesus—by serving others in need. Jesus said in Matthew 25 that whatever we do for others, it's like we're actually doing it for Him. So ask Jesus to show you the people in need whom He wants you to serve. And as you do, ask Him to teach you the wisdom He wants you to learn through the experience.

Dear Jesus, I want to be close to You and learn from You
by serving others in need. Please guide me and give me
a loving, giving heart for others like You have. Amen.

TRUE BEAUTY

Your beauty should come from the inside. It should
come from the heart. This is the kind that lasts.
1 PETER 3:4

We love to shop (especially for good deals!) and find cute clothes to wear and fun accessories to go with them. How about you? Whether you do or not, everyone needs wisdom when we choose our clothes and styles and when we look in the mirror. Does real beauty come from the outside? Definitely not. You might know someone who always wears the coolest clothes and looks super pretty but doesn't act very nice or treat others kindly. Does that seem truly beautiful to you? It definitely should not. And maybe you know someone who never has the latest fashions and who doesn't ever follow the latest trends in hair and makeup, but they have kindness and honesty and love overflowing out of them for others. Does that seem truly beautiful to you? It totally should!

Dear God, please always help me to have the right
idea in my mind about what true beauty is. People look
at the outside, but You look at the heart (1 Samuel 16:7),
and that's how I want to think of what beauty is too. Amen.

Take Good Care,
Part 1

*Growing strong in body is all right but growing in
God-like living is more important. It will not only
help you in this life now but in the next life also.*
1 Timothy 4:8

❦

One way many people become too obsessed with outer appearance these days is in working out and getting in shape. Those are awesome goals to be healthy, and 1 Corinthians 6:19–20 tells us we should want to take good care of our bodies and honor God with them. But physical fitness goals aren't awesome if people take them too far and give them too much attention. Our focus should be on God most of all. First Timothy 4:8 reminds us that growing in healthy relationship with Him so that we do our best to live like Jesus matters not just for life on earth, which is temporary, but for life in heaven, which is forever!

....

*Dear God, please give me wisdom for keeping my
body healthy and strong, and even more importantly,
for keeping my heart, mind, and spirit in a healthy
and strong relationship with You!*

Take Good Care, Part 2

Do you not know that your body is a house of God where the Holy Spirit lives? God gave you His Holy Spirit. Now you belong to God. You do not belong to yourselves. God bought you with a great price. So honor God with your body. You belong to Him.
1 CORINTHIANS 6:19–20

᪥

This scripture can inspire you your whole life to take good care of your body—it's a house for the Holy Spirit of God who loves you like no one else does. You should want to keep your body healthy and special and able to do the good things God has planned for you. You can do that while you're young by keeping yourself clean and choosing more healthy foods than junk foods and being active to keep your body moving and all its parts working well. As you get older, you can continue all those things plus make wise choices about what you do with your body and what you put in it. Keep asking God to help you every day of your life!

Dear God, please remind me every day that my body is a house for Your Holy Spirit. Thank You that You are so close to me. You have given me this body to do the good things You have planned for me here on earth, and I want to take good care of it and honor You with it! Amen.

WISDOM WITH SOCIAL MEDIA

*So be careful how you live. Live as
men who are wise and not foolish.
Make the best use of your time.*
EPHESIANS 5:15–16

Social media is a big deal these days, and although it can be fun, it can also be really bad for you. It's important to have wisdom not to get too caught up in it. Do you have friends who are already totally obsessed with it? Or maybe you're starting to be obsessed with it yourself. If that's the case, you need to let grown-ups help you set limits, and you need to train yourself to set limits. Choose to put down your phone and tablet and do things without a screen involved. And help encourage your friends to do so as well. Read books. Play actual board games. Get involved in sports and activities. Spend time talking in person and just hanging out doing silly good stuff together. Challenge yourself to see how much fun you can have with no social media involved—and if you still want it and it's okay with Mom and Dad, then just be super-duper wise about using it in small amounts of time.

....

*Dear God, it's not cool to ask You for help with
limits on social media, but I am asking anyway.
I want to be wise about this and make the best
use of my time like Your Word tells me to. Amen.*

MOre WISDOM WITH SOCIAL MEDIA

Whatever you say or do, do it in the name of the Lord Jesus.
Give thanks to God the Father through the Lord Jesus.
COLOSSIANS 3:17

You might hear a lot about people being mean and bullying and arguing in nasty ways on social media—or sharing things that are definitely not kid or family friendly, things that would make God sad. Hopefully if you ever do choose to be on social media, you will want absolutely no part of that. None! Make a promise that you will only use it in positive ways that encourage and help others. The world has enough mean and awful stuff going on; no one needs to spread around any extra!

Dear God, show me ways to use social media for good,
to encourage others and share Your truth and love.
Please help me always to stay far away from the
awful stuff on social media. Thank You! Amen.

WISDOM FROM THE BOOK OF RUTH

May the Lord show kindness to you.
RUTH 1:8

The book of Ruth tells a story about a special woman who lived during the time when judges led the nation of Israel. Ruth and her mother-in-law, Naomi, and sister-in-law, Orpah, all lost their husbands, and it was dangerous in Bible times for a woman not to have a man to take care of her. So Naomi urged the younger women to leave her and go back to their homelands and their people there. But Ruth loved her mother-in-law and wanted to stay with her no matter what. She said, "Do not beg me to leave you or turn away from following you. I will go where you go. I will live where you live. Your people will be my people. And your God will be my God" (Ruth 1:16). Ruth wanted to have faith in the one true God of Israel. And if you read the whole story in the book of Ruth in the Bible, you'll see that because of her loyalty, love, and faith, God blessed Ruth far more than she ever thought possible. We should all want to have the same kind of loyalty, love, and faith as Ruth.

....

Dear God, thank You for the book of Ruth. Help me
as I read it and keep coming back to it in the future.
Teach me what You want me to learn from it to
apply to my life and to share with others. Amen.

WISDOM FROM CHURCH

Let us hold on to the hope we say we have and not be changed.
We can trust God that He will do what He promised. Let us
help each other to love others and to do good. Let us not
stay away from church meetings. . . . Comfort each other
as you see the day of His return coming near.
HEBREWS 10:23–25

We hope you have a church you love going to where all of God's Word is taught and where the love and salvation of Jesus are shared and where others are helped to know Jesus and follow Him. And we hope you love being active in that church. Church should never be just a thing you do here and there, when it feels like a good idea, especially around holidays or when you have a new outfit to wear. Now and your whole life, you should want to be a part of a Bible-teaching church to help you grow in wisdom as you learn and give and serve and gain encouragement. The church is made up of all believers in Jesus all around the world, and when you join in a group of believers in a local church near you, you help to spread God's great big kingdom, both now and forever!

....

Dear God, in every stage of my life, help me to
find the church where You want me to grow in
wisdom from You and in love for others! Amen.

WORKING WISELY, PART 1

Whatever work you do, do it with all your heart. Do it for the Lord and not for men. Remember that you will get your reward from the Lord. He will give you what you should receive. You are working for the Lord Christ.

COLOSSIANS 3:23–24

~~~

This scripture gives you wisdom about how to do your work—whether schoolwork or chores—with all your heart! That means doing your very best with a great attitude. But that's not always easy, is it? Some school subjects are super hard or just plain boring. Some chores seem to take forever when you'd rather be having fun. So, it's very important to remember the boss you're working for—yes, you might be working for your teacher who assigned the homework and will give you the grade, and you might be working for your parents who told you what chores to do. But above and beyond those bosses is your ultimate Boss. That's God, and He loves you like crazy. He wants to reward you in all kinds of ways, here on earth and in heaven, when you do any kind of work with your best effort and best attitude in a way that brings honor to Him.

Dear God, please don't let me forget that You are my Boss and You're the very best Boss ever. Help me to do my very best and have a good attitude with any kind of work I have to do. Amen.

WORKING WISELY, PART 2

Call out with joy to the Lord, all the earth. Be glad as you serve the Lord. Come before Him with songs of joy.
PSALM 100:1–2

Here's a great way to work with a good attitude, doing your best—keep nearly constant praise songs going in your head. Turn up the worship music (if you're allowed) while you do chores, and if you can't actually turn up the music, then just keep singing the praise songs you know inside your mind. Remind yourself what a blessing it is to be able to do work and to learn, and thank God for that blessing. There are some people in the world who would love to go to school and to a job but who don't have the abilities or opportunities. Choosing to praise God while you work brings glory to Him and puts your mind in the right place to give you the best kind of attitude, all while getting good things done. That's a win-win-win!

Dear God, thank You for the blessing of being able to work and to learn. When I might be feeling grumpy about the work I need to do, please help me to remember to start singing praise to You with a grateful heart! Amen.

WORKING WISELY, PART 3

For we are God's masterpiece. He has created us anew in Christ Jesus, so we can do the good things he planned for us long ago.
EPHESIANS 2:10 NLT

Hopefully you already have some ideas of the job you want to have and the work you want to do when you grow up. It's good to start dreaming and thinking of the things you're already good at and how those talents might fit into jobs and goals in the future. Most important as you think and dream is to keep asking God to show you the good works He created you to do. The best jobs for you that will make you the happiest and feel the most rewarding will be the ones God has specifically designed you for. He's given you just the right natural talent— and if you let Him lead you, He'll guide you to all the right learning and people and places that He wants for you.

Dear God, thank You for the talents and abilities You have given me. As I keep learning about what I'm good at and growing in knowledge and wisdom, please show me all the good things You have planned for me to do in my life. Amen.

WISDOM FROM THE BOOKS OF 1 AND 2 SAMUEL

*Hannah prayed and said, "My heart is happy
in the Lord. My strength is honored in the Lord."*
1 SAMUEL 2:1

The book of 1 Samuel starts out telling about brave Hannah's prayer for a son and her promise and her faithfulness to God. The book goes on to tell about the life of her son named Samuel who became a prophet of God. Then it tells about bad King Saul's life. And then in 2 Samuel, David becomes king of Israel. He's known as the nation's greatest king, even though he started out as a lowly shepherd boy! But he was very brave (you've probably heard how he defeated the giant Goliath!), and most importantly he loved and had great faith in God. And even though he made lots of mistakes, he was called a man after God's heart. We should make it our goal to be described as girls and women after God's heart!

*Dear God, thank You for the books of 1 and 2 Samuel.
Help me as I read them and keep coming back to them
in the future. Teach me what You want me to learn from
them to apply to my life and to share with others. Amen.*

WISDOM ABOUT YOUR
SAFEST PLACE

My being safe and my honor rest with God.
My safe place is in God, the rock of my strength.
Trust in Him at all times, O people. Pour out your
heart before Him. God is a safe place for us.
PSALM 62:7–8

If you think of your safe place, do you think of the place where you feel most comfortable and relaxed and understood? We feel that way at home with each other, especially on cozy family movie and game nights. Or maybe you think of your safe place as with your best friend you can talk to about anything. Those are good safe places, but we also have to be careful we don't let anything take the place of our very best safe place—God! When we depend too much on other things for safety and comfort, we forget that God is the strongest and most protective, and He should be first in our lives. He is your rock solid, strongest safe place! He is with you anytime and anywhere. Talk to Him, cry out to Him, depend on Him, and trust Him for everything you need.

. . . .

Dear God, You are my solid rock and safe place
everywhere I go, in every situation. Thank You for
giving me comfort and safety, and please help me to
think only of You as my very best safe place. Amen.

WISDOM FROM THE BOOKS OF 1 AND 2 KINGS

The Lord told Israel and Judah of the danger, through all His men who told what would happen in the future. He said, "Turn from your sinful ways and obey My Laws. Keep all the Laws which I gave your fathers, and which I gave to you through My servants and men of God." But they did not listen.
2 KINGS 17:13–14

In 1 and 2 Kings, King David's son, Solomon, became king over the nation of Israel. God blessed him greatly for wanting to be faithful and have wisdom to know God's ways of right and wrong. But by the end of his reign, Solomon made bad choices and did not lead well. When his son took over as king, Israel soon split apart into two different nations, Israel and Judah. Throughout the years and rise and fall of kings, God spoke to the people through the prophets, especially Elijah and Elisha, who performed amazing miracles. But the nations of Israel and Judah did not listen well to the prophets from God, and by the end of 2 Kings both nations were defeated and held captive by other nations.

Dear God, thank You for the books of 1 and 2 Kings. Help me as I read them and keep coming back to them in the future. Teach me what You want me to learn from them to apply to my life and to share with others. Amen.

WISDOM ABOUT BaPTISM

*Jesus came and said to them, ". . . . Go and make
followers of all the nations. Baptize them in the
name of the Father and of the Son and of the Holy
Spirit. Teach them to do all the things I have told you."*
MATTHEW 28:18–20

If you have accepted Jesus as your Savior, you can choose to
be baptized to show other people that you love and follow
Jesus. It's not something you absolutely *have* to do to be saved
and go to heaven forever. The man who died next to Jesus
when He died on the cross never had a chance to be baptized,
and Jesus promised the man he would be with Him that day
in paradise (Luke 23:42–43). But if you do have a chance, it is
right to obey God's Word and follow Jesus' example. Baptism
is a symbol with water to represent washing away your sin and
choosing new life with Jesus. It's a way to show that you want
to obey God and be like Jesus and that you are saved from sin
and are His follower! Christians who get baptized help inspire
others to trust in Jesus as Savior too.

*Dear God, please give me wisdom about baptism. If it's Your will
for me, help me to be brave to choose baptism. I want to show
others how much I love and want to follow You! Amen.*

WISDOM FROM THE BOOKS OF 1 AND 2 CHRONICLES

"If My people who are called by My name put away
their pride and pray, and look for My face, and turn
from their sinful ways, then I will hear from heaven.
I will forgive their sin, and will heal their land."

2 CHRONICLES 7:14

The books of 1 and 2 Chronicles tell about a lot of the same history as in 1 and 2 Samuel and 1 and 2 Kings, but they focus more on the good lessons to learn in that history about loving and following and worshipping God. It's especially cool to learn more about the youngest king of Israel, Josiah. He wasn't even ten years old! From 2 Chronicles 34, we learn that "Josiah. . . ruled thirty-one years in Jerusalem. He did what was right in the eyes of the Lord, and walked in the ways of his father David." (vv. 1–2). That's pretty cool that such a young kid knew how important it was to follow God. He did many great things to help his nation to love and obey only the one true God of Israel. We should want to be a lot like King Josiah!

....

Dear God, thank You for the books of 1 and 2 Chronicles.
Help me as I read them and keep coming back to them
in the future. Teach me what You want me to learn from
them to apply to my life and to share with others. Amen.

WISDOM WHEN YOU'RE ANGRY, PART 1

If you are angry, do not let it become sin.
Get over your anger before the day is finished.
EPHESIANS 4:26

⚡

We definitely get angry with each other in our family some-times, and we don't always handle our anger well. We sure need God's help and wisdom! The Bible doesn't say anger is always bad; God knows we will and should be angry sometimes. But the Bible does say not to sin when we are angry. That's super hard to obey sometimes! The moment we feel anger start to rise up inside our hearts and minds, we need to train ourselves to take big deep breaths and slow down, then pray and ask God how we should react. Proverbs 14:29 says, "He who is slow to get angry has great understanding, but he who has a quick temper makes his foolish way look right." And James 1:19 (NIV) says, "Everyone should be quick to listen, slow to speak and slow to become angry."

. . . .

Dear God, please help me slow down when I start to feel angry.
Help me to stop and pray to You for wisdom on how to handle
it. I don't want to sin when I am angry; I want to deal with
it in ways that honor You and share Your love. Amen.

WISDOM WHEN YOU'RE ANGRY, PART 2

*God has chosen you. You are holy and loved by Him.
Because of this, your new life should be full of loving-pity.
You should be kind to others and have no pride. Be gentle and
be willing to wait for others. Try to understand other people.
Forgive each other. If you have something against someone,
forgive him. That is the way the Lord forgave you. And to all
these things, you must add love. Love holds everything and
everybody together and makes all these good things perfect.*
COLOSSIANS 3:12–14

Think of specific things that have made you angry, and then think of ways you could replace the anger with something good. What if a sibling or friend acts mean and picks a fight with you for no reason? You could choose to keep a fight going, or you could choose to be a peacemaker and suggest something fun to do together instead of fighting. If the sibling or friend won't stop, then you can choose to walk away and/or calmly get a grown-up to help. Let God help you with all kinds of situations that make you angry. He can help you find a way to turn them into something good.

*Dear God, please help me when I'm mad. I want
to make the situation better, not worse. Amen.*

WISDOM FROM THE BOOK OF EZRA

Ezra had set his heart to learn the Law of the Lord,
to live by it, and to teach His Laws in Israel.
EZRA 7:10

In the beginning of the book of Ezra, King Cyrus of Persia decided to allow the Jews who had been captive to return to their homeland in Israel. A group of them, led by a man named Zerubbabel, went back to Jerusalem to rebuild the temple, which had been destroyed seventy years earlier. In the last four chapters, the book of Ezra also tells about the life and ministry of a man named Ezra, who was a priest, or religious leader, who loved to learn and live by and teach God's Word. He is a great example of wisdom and faithfulness to God for all who choose to learn from his life.

Dear God, thank You for the book of Ezra. Help me
as I read it and keep coming back to it in the future.
Teach me what You want me to learn from it to apply
to my life and to share with others. Amen.

WISDOM ABOUT GOD'S GRACE

Are we to keep on sinning so that God will
give us more of His loving-favor? No, not at all!
ROMANS 6:1–2

When we ask God for forgiveness from the things we do wrong, He is so good and loving! He forgives fully and well! So sometimes we might think it's no big deal to keep doing sinful things and then just ask for forgiveness. But that's not a good and wise way to think at all. If we truly love God, we want to obey Him and honor Him, not choose bad things again and again with a "who cares?" attitude. We are absolutely going to mess up and make bad choices sometimes, but we should feel sad about that and how it hurts God. Then we should do our best to avoid more sin in the future. Also, even while God always forgives when we ask, He doesn't always keep us from the consequences that go along with sin. Ask God to help you to keep running away from sin, not playing around with it like it doesn't matter.

. . . .

Dear God, I know You love me no matter what, but I don't
want to sin against You on purpose whenever I want and
pretend it's no big deal. Please help me to keep growing
in wisdom about Your wonderful grace. Amen.

WISDOM FROM THE BOOK OF NEHEMIAH

"O Lord, hear the prayer of Your servant and the prayer of Your servants who are happy to fear Your name."
NEHEMIAH 1:11

In the book of Nehemiah, we learn a lot about a Jewish man named Nehemiah who served as the cupbearer for the Persian king Artaxerxes. His job was to taste all the king's food and drink before the king did to make sure no one was trying to poison the king with it. The king liked Nehemiah, so when Nehemiah wanted to go back to his homeland and help build the walls around Jerusalem, the king let him. Nehemiah organized and led a team of builders, and within fifty-two days they were able to rebuild the city's walls. That was incredibly fast for such a big job, and it showed how God's power was clearly at work. Nehemiah loved and respected God with all of his heart, and he continued to help the Jewish people want to honor and obey Him in all things.

Dear God, thank You for the book of Nehemiah. Help me as I read it and keep coming back to it in the future. Teach me what You want me to learn from it to apply to my life and to share with others. Amen.

WISDOM ABOUT THE ONE TRUE RELIGION

We need such a Religious Leader Who made the way for man to go to God. Jesus is holy and has no guilt. He has never sinned and is different from sinful men. He has the place of honor above the heavens. . . . [Christ] gave one gift on the altar and that gift was Himself. It was done once and it was for all time.
HEBREWS 7:26–27

You might hear people say that all religions are the same, and you need wisdom about that, because it's just not true. Belief in Jesus as God and our one and only Savior is the truth. Jesus was the only human being to live on earth who was holy and without any sin. He gave His own life to die once for all people of all time to save them from their sin—and then He rose again to show His power over death and offer eternal life to all who trust in Him. No other religion offers that kind of gift and love and miracle! To know Jesus as Savior is simply to believe in Him and accept the awesome gift of grace and eternal life he gave when He took our sins away by dying on the cross and rising to life again.

Dear Jesus, thank You for giving Your life to save everyone who believes in You! You are God and You are our one and only living Savior! Amen.

WISDOM FROM THE BOOK OF ESTHER

*Queen Esther answered, "If I have found favor
in your eyes, O king, and if it please the king, I ask
that my life and the lives of my people be saved."*
ESTHER 7:3

In the book of Esther, we learn that when King Xerxes of Persia
began searching for a new queen, he liked Esther best. She was
a Jewish woman, but she had kept her family history a secret.
A high official in the land named Haman wanted all people to
bow down and honor him, but Esther's cousin Mordecai refused to bow down to anyone but God. Because of this, Haman
was filled with hate for Jewish people, and he convinced King
Xerxes to order a decree to have them all killed. But Esther
had great courage, and she asked the king to have mercy on
the Jews. When you read the whole account in the Bible, you
learn how Esther let God work through her to save her entire
nation of people.

*Dear God, thank You for the book of Esther. Help me
as I read it and keep coming back to it in the future.
Teach me what You want me to learn from it to apply
to my life and to share with others. Amen.*

WISDOM TO CONQUER FEAR, PART 1

Show me Your loving-kindness, O God. . . .
When I am afraid, I will trust in You.
PSALM 56:1, 3

Can you think of a fear you used to have but then you got over it? What happened? How did God help you? Who were the people and things He provided to get you through it? It's wise to take time every once in a while to focus on things you used to be afraid of that now seem like no big deal. It helps you realize that whatever is making you scared or nervous today will probably one day be no big deal either. God never leaves you alone. He is right there with you in the middle of your fears, and you can call out for His help at any time. He will guide you through it to the other side where you can look back with relief and say, "Wow! Thanks, God! We conquered that together, and now I'm not afraid anymore!"

. . . .

Dear God, please help me with these fears I have: _____.
I remember all the ways You have helped me conquer fears
in the past, and I am trusting that You will help again
now and always in the future too. Amen.

WISDOM TO CONQUER FEAR, PART 2

*Wait for the LORD; be strong, and let your
heart take courage; wait for the LORD!*
PSALM 27:14 ESV

Sometimes you have to wait on God to help you conquer a fear. In those times, keep focusing on Him through scripture and prayer and praise. Read and memorize scripture about fear like these and repeat them, pray them, and sing them. When your mind is focused on God, it doesn't have time to focus on fear.

- "Even if I walk through the valley of the shadow of death, I will not be afraid of anything, because You are with me" (Psalm 23:4).

- "The Lord is my light and the One Who saves me. Whom should I fear? The Lord is the strength of my life. Of whom should I be afraid?" (Psalm 27:1).

- "God is our safe place and our strength. He is always our help when we are in trouble. So we will not be afraid, even if the earth is shaken and the mountains fall into the center of the sea, and even if its waters go wild with storm and the mountains shake with its action" (Psalm 46:1–3).

Dear God, please help me to keep my mind thinking about You, praying to You, and praising You when I feel afraid. I am waiting on You and trusting in You to help me conquer every fear. Amen.

WISDOM TO CONQUER FEAR, PART 3

*The Holy Writings say, "Because of belonging to Jesus,
we are in danger of being killed all day long. We are thought
of as sheep that are ready to be killed." But we have power
over all these things through Jesus Who loves us so much.*
ROMANS 8:36–37

Wow, that's quite a fear this scripture talks about—being afraid all day long of being killed! Hopefully the fears you need to conquer are not quite that scary, but maybe they feel just as bad sometimes. If they do, be sure to keep reading in Romans 8, because that passage goes on to tell you exactly why you have power over anything that puts you in danger or scares you—it's because absolutely *nothing* can keep the love of God away from you! He will always be with you, taking care of you. Romans 8:38–39 says, "Death cannot! Life cannot! Angels cannot! Leaders cannot! Any other power cannot! Hard things now or in the future cannot! The world above or the world below cannot! Any other living thing cannot keep us away from the love of God which is ours through Christ Jesus our Lord."

*Dear God, I don't ever want to forget that absolutely nothing
can keep Your love away from me. Thank You so much for being
so powerful in me to overcome any kind of fear. Amen.*

WHEN Fear Can BE a GOOD THING

Good thinking will keep you safe. Understanding will watch over you. You will be kept from the sinful man, and from the man who causes much trouble by what he says. You will be kept from the man who leaves the right way to walk in the ways of darkness.

PROVERBS 2:11–13

It's good to remember that sometimes fear can be good for you. It can keep you out of danger and trouble. You don't have to fear a backyard campfire, but you should fear fire in the sense that you know you should never play around with it and start a big out-of-control blaze. Also, you should fear what would happen if you listened to some friends who wanted to disobey the rules and sneak out of school sometime. That's a good fear to listen to, because you sure don't want to get in big trouble for that. God can use fear to direct you away from what would be harmful or foolish or troublesome for you, so keep on asking Him for wisdom to show you the times when it's good to listen to fear.

Dear God, please help me to know when fear is good for me because You're using it to keep me safe and out of trouble. Thank You for watching over me so well! Amen.

WISDOM FROM THE
BOOK OF JOB

*"The Lord gave and the Lord has taken away.
Praise the name of the Lord."*
JOB 1:21

The book of Job is a story about a very rich man from the land of Uz named Job. (His name rhymes with *robe*.) He was a very good man who had great faith in God. He had a wife and a large family and lots of livestock. He was called the greatest man among all the people of the East. But then God allowed our enemy, Satan, to take everything from Job, including his children, and cause him to suffer. Still, Job loved and praised and followed God. God reminded Job of His great power and goodness, and Job recognized his wrong thinking. Job was sorry and prayed for forgiveness, and God listened and forgave him—and then God restored to Job all he had lost plus much, much more! When we learn from Job's story, we gain wisdom to help us in our sufferings too.

....

*Dear God, thank You for the book of Job. Help me
as I read it and keep coming back to it in the future.
Teach me what You want me to learn from it to
apply to my life and to share with others. Amen.*

KEEP LOOKING TO JESUS

*Let us put every thing out of our lives that keeps us
from doing what we should. Let us keep running in
the race that God has planned for us. Let us keep
looking to Jesus. Our faith comes from Him
and He is the One Who makes it perfect.*
HEBREWS 12:1–2

There are so many cool things to do in life, but we sure can't do them all. It's just not possible! So we need wisdom from God to choose the best things He has for us in the midst of the many good things. And there are lots of bad things to stay far away from too. So the best way to live is to keep looking to Jesus, keep reading His Word, keep praying to Him and asking Him to show you the race God has mapped out specifically for you. Jesus is our example because He lived a perfect life and did exactly what God had planned for Him, and now He is sitting in the very best place in heaven forever!

....

*Dear Jesus, I want to keep looking to You
and following Your example for wisdom.
Please keep showing me the good race
God has mapped out for me. Amen.*

72

WISDOM FROM THE BOOK OF PSALMS

Praise the Lord, all nations! Praise Him, all people!
For His loving-kindness toward us is great. And the
truth of the Lord lasts forever. Praise the Lord!
PSALM 117

The book of Psalms is the longest book of the Bible with 150 chapters! It's a big collection of songs and poems and writings in which the authors are praising and worshipping, praying and crying out to God with all kinds of emotions we can relate to. As we read them, they can lead us in good praise and worship and help guide us in our prayers and crying out to God too.

Dear God, thank You for the book of Psalms. Help me
as I read it and keep coming back to it in the future.
Teach me what You want me to learn from it to apply
to my life and to share with others. Amen.

WISDOM FROM THE GREATEST COMMANDMENTS

"Teacher, which one is the greatest of the Laws?" Jesus said to him, " 'You must love the Lord your God with all your heart and with all your soul and with all your mind.' This is the first and greatest of the Laws. The second is like it, 'You must love your neighbor as you love yourself.' All the Laws and the writings of the early preachers depend on these two most important Laws."
MATTHEW 22:36–40

Knowing and following the commandments that Jesus said are the most important to obey is definitely wise! He said the greatest command is to love God with all your heart, soul, and mind. And the second is to love your neighbor as yourself. If you put these things on the top of your list every moment of every day, you will automatically do other things well too. Because as you love God with all your heart, soul, and mind, you will be wanting to learn more and more about Him. And as you constantly learn about Him and grow closer to Him plus love others as you love yourself, you'll find yourself living the awesome life He has planned for you!

Dear God, I want wisdom about Your greatest commandments. Help me to follow them and love You and others more and more and more each day! Amen.

BE WISE AND BE KIND, PART 1

Your kindness will reward you,
but your cruelty will destroy you.
PROVERBS 11:17 NLT

A girl who is wise knows that being mean to others never does any good. If you've ever acted like a mean girl, you need to admit your sin, apologize, and make it right and work toward doing better at choosing kindness. God loves and forgives you! Here's what God's Word says about kindness and doing good to others to help us:

- "Love is kind" (1 Corinthians 13:4).

- "Do not let yourselves get tired of doing good. If we do not give up, we will get what is coming to us at the right time. Because of this, we should do good to everyone. For sure, we should do good to those who belong to Christ" (Galatians 6:9–10).

- "We know what real love is because Jesus gave up his life for us. So we also ought to give up our lives for our brothers and sisters. If someone has enough money to live well and sees a brother or sister in need but shows no compassion—how can God's love be in that person? Dear children, let's not merely say that we love each other; let us show the truth by our actions" (1 John 3:16–18 NLT).

Dear God, help me always to be wise to know that being kind rewards me but being mean destroys me. Please fill me with Your real love and goodness to share with others. Amen.

BE WISE AND BE KIND, PART 2

We who have strong faith should help those who
are weak. . . . Each of us should live to please
his neighbor. This will help him grow in faith.
ROMANS 15:1–2

~~~~

Being kind to others doesn't mean you have to be close friends
with every person around you. That would be impossible! And
even trying to be friends with every person is not wise, because if you did, you'd never have time for everyone and for
the good things God has planned for you. Plus the Bible tells
us there are people we should never want to be close friends
with, like angry ones described in Proverbs 22:24–25.

Being kind to others also doesn't mean you have to agree
with them about everything. You can agree to disagree and
still show kindness and respect. When you focus on the fact
that every single person in the world (no matter who they are
or what they do or what their personality is like) is created and
loved by God, He will help you to be kind and respectful to
anyone who comes into your life. Ask God to help you to grow
in kindness, and He will help you share kindness in wise and
loving ways.

. . . .

Dear God, please help me to remember all people
are so loved by You and to treat everyone kindly and
respectfully. Give me wisdom about sharing kindness
and love with those You have planned for me to. Amen.

WISDOM FROM THE BOOK OF PROVERBS

These are the wise sayings of Solomon, son of David, king of Israel: They show you how to know wisdom and teaching, to find the words of understanding. They help you learn about the ways of wisdom and what is right and fair. They give wisdom to the child-like, and much learning and wisdom to those who are young. A wise man will hear and grow in learning. A man of understanding will become able to understand a saying and a picture-story, the words of the wise and what they mean.

PROVERBS 1:1–6

The book of Proverbs is all about wisdom! It's a big collection of short sayings and thoughts and tips to help people of all ages in all kinds of situations choose right instead of wrong by following God's good ways. It's really neat how there are thirty-one chapters since most of our months have thirty-one days. It's super wise to read one chapter of Proverbs every day of the month and then start all over again the next month.

. . . .

Dear God, thank You for the book of Proverbs. Help me as I read it and keep coming back to it in the future. Teach me what You want me to learn from it to apply to my life and to share with others. Amen.

WISDOM ABOUT WEALTH

*A God-like life gives us much when we are happy for
what we have. We came into this world with nothing.
For sure, when we die, we will take nothing with us. If we
have food and clothing, let us be happy. But men who want
lots of money are tempted. They are trapped into doing all
kinds of foolish things and things which hurt them. These
things drag them into sin and will destroy them. The love of
money is the beginning of all kinds of sin. Some people have
turned from the faith because of their love for money. They
have made much pain for themselves because of this.*
1 TIMOTHY 6:6–10

A lot of people make their goals in life based on what will help
them gain more money, and that's not wise at all. Choose now
while you are young not to make that your focus. Instead, trust
God's Word that getting trapped in wanting lots of money can
lead to all kinds of sin and foolish things. Let Him help you
focus on goals that match up with His good plans for your life.

....

*Dear God, please give me wisdom about wealth.
I don't want my goals to be about money; I want
them to be about serving You and doing the
good things You have planned for me! Amen.*

WISDOM FROM THE BOOK
OF ECCLESIASTES

The last word, after all has been heard, is:
Honor God and obey His Laws. This is all that
every person must do. For God will judge every act,
even everything which is hidden, both good and bad.
ECCLESIASTES 12:13–14

The writer of the book of Ecclesiastes was most likely King Solomon, the king whom God was so happy with when he asked for wisdom. But remember that King Solomon didn't continue using wisdom later on in his life, and some Bible experts think he wrote Ecclesiastes to help teach other people the lessons he learned from his bad choices. We are wise when we listen to those who have made mistakes and learned from them, because hopefully we won't make the same mistakes!

Dear God, thank You for the book of Ecclesiastes.
Help me as I read it and keep coming back to it in
the future. Teach me what You want me to learn from
it to apply to my life and to share with others. Amen.

DON'T HOLD ON TO ANGER

Put out of your life all these things: bad feelings about other people, anger, temper, loud talk, bad talk which hurts other people, and bad feelings which hurt other people. You must be kind to each other. Think of the other person. Forgive other people just as God forgave you because of Christ's death on the cross.
EPHESIANS 4:31–32

Have you ever gotten angry when your parents promised something fun, but then plans had to change because of a stressful situation? Maybe your family had to cancel vacation because of illness or there was no money for the dance lessons you wanted because of a job loss for Dad or Mom. Of course you'll feel upset about those kinds of things, but you can hold on to anger, or you can be forgiving, understanding, and loving when your family is going through a hard time. The first choice will just make a bad situation worse, but the second will encourage and bless you and everyone around you.

Dear God, when I'm disappointed and angry that plans have to change, please help me to choose a good attitude, with forgiveness, understanding, and love. Amen.

WISDOM FROM THE BOOK OF SONG OF SOLOMON

The Song of Songs, the most beautiful of them all, which is Solomon's.
SONG OF SOLOMON 1:1

Song of Solomon, or Song of Songs as it's also called, is a book about the beauty of married love. Some Bible experts think it was written (either by Solomon or about him) as a way to compare married love with how much God loves His people. He loves us all far more than we can even imagine!

· ·

Dear God, thank You for the Song of Solomon. Help me as I read it and keep coming back to it in the future. Teach me what You want me to learn from it to apply to my life and to share with others. Amen.

WISDOM ABOUT TROUBLES, Part 1

Troubles help us learn not to give up. When we have learned not to give up, it shows we have stood the test. When we have stood the test, it gives us hope. Hope never makes us ashamed because the love of God has come into our hearts through the Holy Spirit Who was given to us.
ROMANS 5:3–5

What would it look like to you if everything about life was always easy and fun? Would you always be on vacation with no homework or tests to take or chores to do, no fighting with siblings or friends, no bedtime, no sickness or death? All that sounds pretty great, but it's wise to know that a trouble-free life is sadly just not possible because of sin in the world. But the good news is, God is using the troubles for good, and His Word promises that "the little troubles we suffer now for a short time are making us ready for the great things God is going to give us forever. We do not look at the things that can be seen. We look at the things that cannot be seen. The things that can be seen will come to an end. But the things that cannot be seen will last forever" (2 Corinthians 4:17–18).

Dear God, please help me to expect troubles and learn from them as I trust that You are turning them into good things for me. Amen.

WISDOM ABOUT TROUBLES, PArt 2

You are being kept by the power of God because you put your trust in Him and you will be saved from the punishment of sin at the end of the world. With this hope you can be happy even if you need to have sorrow and all kinds of tests for awhile. These tests have come to prove your faith and to show that it is good. Gold, which can be destroyed, is tested by fire. Your faith is worth much more than gold and it must be tested also. Then your faith will bring thanks and shining-greatness and honor to Jesus Christ when He comes again.
1 PETER 1:5–7

We can find all kinds of wisdom in the Bible to help us deal with troubles, like this wisdom in 1 Peter 1 that reminds us that how we react to our troubles helps prove our faith in God. If we say we have faith in God *only* when times are good, then that faith isn't real. But if we hold to our faith even when times are bad, we prove that we love and believe in God no matter what!

Dear God, please help me to remember that hard times prove whether I truly love and believe in You. I want to show You and everyone around me that my faith in You is real and strong! Amen.

WISDOM FROM THE BOOK OF ISAIAH

*For sure He took on Himself our troubles and carried our
sorrows. Yet we thought of Him as being punished and hurt by
God, and made to suffer. But He was hurt for our wrong-doing.
He was crushed for our sins. He was punished so we would have
peace. He was beaten so we would be healed. All of us like sheep
have gone the wrong way. Each of us has turned to his own way.
And the Lord has put on Him the sin of us all.*

Isaiah 53:4–6

The book of Isaiah is the first in a series of seventeen books
written by prophets. They are books that warn about God's
judgment and also give encouragement with the promises of
God's salvation and forgiveness and the way He rescues when
people turn back to Him. Isaiah is extra special among the pro-
phetic books because it has more prophecies about our Savior
Jesus than any of the others!

*Dear God, thank You for the book of Isaiah. Help me
as I read it and keep coming back to it in the future.
Teach me what You want me to learn from it to apply
to my life and to share with others. Amen.*

WISDOM FROM JESUS' STORIES

The followers of Jesus came to Him and said,
"Why do You speak to them in picture-stories?"
MATTHEW 13:10

When Jesus lived on earth and taught people about God, He often used parables, or "picture-stories." His followers asked Him why He taught people this way, and He said: "This is why I speak to them in picture-stories. They have eyes but they do not see. They have ears but they do not hear and they do not understand. It happened in their lives as Isaiah said it would happen. He said, 'You hear and hear but do not understand. You look and look but do not see. . . . They hear very little with their ears. They have closed their eyes. If they did not do this, they would see with their eyes and hear with their ears and understand with their hearts. Then they would be changed in their ways, and I would heal them' " (Matthew 13:13–15).

Remember this answer from Jesus and be praying for great wisdom and understanding as you study His stories and His example and all the writings in the whole Bible. We want to have eyes and ears and hearts that are open and paying attention to understand how God is trying to teach and guide and love us.

. . . .

Dear God, please give me great wisdom and understanding
as I read Your Word and learn from Jesus. Help me and guide
me and change any of my ways that need changing. Amen.

GOOD GrOUND

"When anyone hears the Word about the holy nation and does not understand it, the devil comes and takes away what was put in his heart. He is like the seed that fell by the side of the road. The seed which fell between rocks is like the person who receives the Word with joy as soon as he hears it. Its root is not deep and it does not last long. When troubles and suffering come because of the Word, he gives up and falls away. The seed which fell among thorns is like the person who hears the Word but the cares of this life, and the love for money let the thorns come up and do not give the seed room to grow and give grain. The seed which fell on good ground is like the one who hears the Word and understands it. He gives much grain. Some seed gives one hundred times as much grain. Some gives sixty times as much grain. Some gives thirty times as much grain."

MATTHEW 13:19–23

⤜⤜⤜

This picture-story or parable from Jesus gives us wisdom about what happens among different types of people who hear God's truth from His Word. We should always want to be like the last kind of people described—those who hear God's Word and understand it so that we can grow more good things in our lives that honor God and spread even more of His truth and love.

....

Dear God, please help my heart and mind and my whole life be "good ground" where Your wisdom and truth grow and multiply! Amen.

WISDOM FROM THE BOOK OF JEREMIAH

*The Word of the Lord came to me saying, "Before I started
to put you together in your mother, I knew you. Before
you were born, I set you apart as holy. I chose you to speak
to the nations for Me." Then I said, "O, Lord God! I do not
know how to speak. I am only a boy." But the Lord said to me,
"Do not say, 'I am only a boy.' You must go everywhere I send
you. And you must say whatever I tell you. Do not be afraid
of them. For I am with you to take you out of trouble."*

JEREMIAH 1:4–8

After King Josiah died, the nation of Judah had turned almost
completely away from God. So in his book, the prophet Jeremiah warned the people of Judah of the punishment and
suffering that was about to come their way because of their
rejection of God and His good ways. The book reminds us
never to reject God and His good ways. He always wants what
is best for us!

*Dear God, thank You for the book of Jeremiah. Help me
as I read it and keep coming back to it in the future.
Teach me what You want me to learn from it to apply
to my life and to share with others. Amen.*

Jesus' Wisdom About Little Children

[Jesus] said, "For sure, I tell you, unless you. . .become like a little child, you will not get into the holy nation of heaven. Whoever is without pride as this little child is the greatest in the holy nation of heaven. Whoever receives a little child because of Me receives Me."
MATTHEW 18:3–5

Jesus taught His followers about how much He loves and values little children and how we need to be like them. Then He went on to teach in a parable about the lost sheep to show that God loves His children and never wants even one to be lost: "For the Son of Man has come to save that which was lost. What do you think about this? A man has one hundred sheep and one of them is lost. Will he not leave the ninety-nine and go to the mountains to look for that one lost sheep? If he finds it, for sure, I tell you, he will have more joy over that one, than over the ninety-nine that were not lost. I tell you, My Father in heaven does not want one of these little children to be lost" (Matthew 18:11–14).

Dear Jesus, thank You for teaching Your wisdom about children and Your great love for us! Thank You for never wanting me or anyone to be lost! Amen.

WHY DO BAD THINGS HAPPEN?

We know that we belong to God, but the whole world is under the power of the devil. We know God's Son has come. He has given us the understanding to know Him Who is the true God. We are joined together with the true God through His Son, Jesus Christ. He is the true God and the life that lasts forever. My children, keep yourselves from false gods.
1 JOHN 5:19–21

You might wonder sometimes why bad things happen in this world, especially when you're in the middle of something bad happening to you. It's because the whole world is under the power of the devil. But for all of us who believe in Jesus as Savior, we belong to God and the devil can never defeat us. The devil can attack us and hurt us, but God gives us life that lasts forever, no matter what! We should never want to follow any other type of false god who will lead us into the ways of the devil. Only the one true God leads us to life that lasts forever.

Dear God, please give me extra love and wisdom when bad things happen and I don't totally understand. I trust that with Jesus as my Savior, no matter what happens to me, You give me life that lasts forever! Amen.

WISDOM FROM THE BOOK OF LAMENTATIONS

*My eyes become weak from crying. My spirit is
very troubled. My heart is poured out in sorrow,
because my people have been destroyed.*
LAMENTATIONS 2:11

Lamentations, written by the prophet Jeremiah, is a super sad book. A lamentation is an expression of sorrow, such as a sad poem or song or journal entry. Sometimes when you feel sad about something, it can be really helpful to write down all your sad feelings as you tell God about them and let Him comfort you. You can share them with trusted loved ones in your life too. In the book of Lamentations, Jeremiah was writing down all of his sadness about the way the city of Jerusalem had been destroyed (just like God had told him to warn about in his first book) because the people had turned away from God.

*Dear God, thank You for the book of Lamentations.
Help me as I read it and keep coming back to it in
the future. Teach me what You want me to learn from
it to apply to my life and to share with others. Amen.*

LOVe FOr NeiGHBOrS

He asked Jesus, "Who is my neighbor?"
LUKE 10:29

Jesus taught wisdom about loving others in this parable:

"A man was going down from Jerusalem to the city of Jericho. Robbers. . .took his clothes off and beat him. . . leaving him almost dead. A religious leader. . .saw the man. But he went by. . . . A man from the family group of Levi. . .saw the man [and] kept on going on the other side of the road. Then a man from the country of Samaria came by. . . . As he saw him, he had loving-pity on him. He got down and put oil and wine on the places where he was hurt and put cloth around them. Then the man from Samaria put this man on his own donkey. He took him to a place where people stay for the night and cared for him. The next day the man from Samaria . . .gave the owner of that place two pieces of money to care for him. He said to him, 'Take care of this man. If you use more than this, I will give it to you when I come again.'

"Which of these three do you think was a neighbor to the man who was beaten by the robbers?" The man who knew the Law said, "The one who showed loving-pity on him." Then Jesus said, "Go and do the same." (Luke 10:30–37)

. . . .

Dear Jesus, help me to love and care for others,
no matter who they are, just like You taught. Amen.

WISDOM FROM THE BOOK OF EZEKIEL

"As I live," says the Lord God, "I am not pleased when sinful
people die. But I am pleased when the sinful turn from
their way and live. Turn! Turn from your sinful ways!"
EZEKIEL 33:11

Ezekiel was a prophet whose name means "strengthened by God." He preached to the people of his day about God's judgment and salvation. Sometimes God told Ezekiel to do some pretty weird-sounding things to demonstrate the warnings God wanted the people to hear. For example, when Ezekiel was told to lie on his left side for 390 days, that was to show the nation of Israel it would be punished for 390 years for turning away from God. However, as Ezekiel 33:11 shows us, God is never happy when people are punished for their sins. He wants people to turn away from them and let Him give them life, the best kind of life of faith in and obedience to Him.

Dear God, thank You for the book of Ezekiel. Help me
as I read it and keep coming back to it in the future.
Teach me what You want me to learn from it to apply
to my life and to share with others. Amen.

BUBBLE BRAIN, PART 1

Keep your minds thinking about whatever is true, whatever is respected, whatever is right, whatever is pure, whatever can be loved, and whatever is well thought of. If there is anything good and worth giving thanks for, think about these things.
PHILIPPIANS 4:8

This scripture is not always easy to obey. If we're honest, we often have thoughts in our mind that are the opposite of what is right, pure, lovely, good, and grateful. On grumpy days and when things go wrong or when someone is mean to you, your first thought isn't usually a happy, thankful one. But God wants you to try to get rid of bad thoughts and keep your mind thinking positively. When you focus on praise and gratitude to Him most of all and on the many things that are right and true in your life, you keep your thoughts in the best places. When negative and nasty thoughts try to take over your mind, think of popping them like a bubble to make them disappear. Then blow positive bubbles into your brain that are strong and healthy for you because they are full of God's goodness and love.

· ·

Dear God, please help me to keep my brain thinking about what is good for me—most of all You because You are so awesome! Amen.

BUBBLE BRAIN, PART 2

Do not act like the sinful people of the world. Let God change your life. First of all, let Him give you a new mind. Then you will know what God wants you to do. And the things you do will be good and pleasing and perfect.
ROMANS 12:2

God wants to give you a new mind full of good thoughts that are focused on Him and are wise and right and true! Check out all these verses that will help you want to train your brain to think about God and what He wants for you more than anything else:

- "If your sinful old self is the boss over your mind, it leads to death. But if the Holy Spirit is the boss over your mind, it leads to life and peace" (Romans 8:6).

- "You will keep the man in perfect peace whose mind is kept on You, because he trusts in You" (Isaiah 26:3).

- "If then you have been raised with Christ, keep looking for the good things of heaven. This is where Christ is seated on the right side of God. Keep your minds thinking about things in heaven" (Colossians 3:1–2).

....

Dear God, please be the boss over my mind through Your Holy Spirit. Please keep me in perfect peace and on the good paths You have for me because I want to think about You and follow You! Amen.

WISDOM FROM THE BOOK OF DANIEL

God gave these four young men much learning and understanding in all kinds of writings and wisdom. Daniel even had understanding in all kinds of special dreams.
DANIEL 1:17

The book of Daniel has several amazing Bible stories you might recognize—like the account of Daniel being thrown into the den of lions because he refused to stop praying to God. And the account of Daniel's friends Shadrach, Meshach, and Abednego, who were thrown into a fiery furnace because they would not bow down to a false god. These true accounts and others about faithfulness to God, even in the worst and scariest of situations, can help you to be strong and brave in your faith as well.

Dear God, thank You for the book of Daniel. Help me as I read it and keep coming back to it in the future. Teach me what You want me to learn from it to apply to my life and to share with others. Amen.

WHEN YOU'RE TEASED ABOUT YOUR FAITH

*If men speak bad of you because you are a Christian,
you will be happy because the Spirit of shining-greatness
and of God is in you. . . . But if a man suffers as a
Christian, he should not be ashamed. He should
thank God that he is a Christian.*
1 PETER 4:14, 16

If you are ever teased for being a Christian, you can think about it with wisdom and be happy about it! Maybe that sounds silly, but God's Word tells us we should not be ashamed; we should be thankful instead! It means God's Spirit is in you and that you are saved forever, so don't worry about what anyone else might say to tease you or be mean to you. Matthew 5:11–12 (NLT) says, "God blesses you when people mock you and per-secute you and lie about you and say all sorts of evil things against you because you are my followers. Be happy about it! Be very glad! For a great reward awaits you in heaven."

Dear Jesus, help me not to get angry or ashamed if people tease me or act mean because I love and follow You. Give me wisdom about what the Bible says. Remind me to be happy because You have saved me and my rewards will be great in heaven. Amen.

WISDOM FROM THE
BOOK OF HOSEA

*"Come, let us return to the Lord. He has hurt us but He
will heal us. He has cut us but He will cover the sore.
After two days He will give us new life. He will raise
us up on the third day, that we may live before Him.
So keep on trying to know the Lord. His coming to us is as
sure as the rising of the sun. He will come to us like the
rain, like the spring rain giving water to the earth."*
HOSEA 6:1–3

The book of Hosea tells how the prophet Hosea, whose name means "salvation," obeyed God's instructions to marry a woman named Gomer, who was not faithful to him. But God told Hosea to go win her back when she ran away. God used this to illustrate how even while the people of Israel were unfaithful to God, God still loved them and wanted to win them back to Him.

*Dear God, thank You for the book of Hosea. Help me
as I read it and keep coming back to it in the future.
Teach me what You want me to learn from it to apply
to my life and to share with others. Amen.*

JESUS' WISDOM
ABOUT THE RICH MAN

*"The fields of a rich man gave much grain. The rich man thought
to himself, 'What will I do? I have no place to put the grain.' Then
he said, 'I know what I will do. I will take down my grain building
and I will build a bigger one. I will put all my grain and other
things I own into it. And I will say to my soul, "Soul, you have
many good things put away in your building. It will be all you
need for many years to come. Now rest and eat and drink and
have lots of fun.'" But God said to him, 'You fool! Tonight your
soul will be taken from you. Then who will have all the things
you have put away?' It is the same with a man who puts away
riches for himself and does not have the riches of God."*
LUKE 12:16–21

Jesus shared this parable to teach us that when we have a lot,
we should be willing to share it with others. No person has any
idea exactly how many days they will live on this earth. It's far
better to be generous to others than to store it all up selfishly.
Our goal should be to have the riches of God, not the riches
of this world.

. . . .

*Dear God, help me to remember Your wisdom and
never be selfish with my money and possessions.
Please give me a heart that loves to share. Amen.*

WISDOM FROM THE
BOOK OF JOEL

*I will show powerful works in the heavens and on
the earth, like blood and fire and clouds of smoke.
The sun will turn dark and the moon will turn to blood
before the day of the Lord. His coming will be a great and
troubled day. It will be that whoever calls on the name
of the Lord will be saved from the punishment of sin.*
JOEL 2:30–32

In the book of Joel, God uses grasshoppers and His message through the prophet Joel to warn the nation of Israel to turn back to Him. Grasshoppers might seem like no big deal, but a huge swarm of them could ruin crops and cause famine and starvation and devastation for a whole nation of people. They were an example of God's judgment on sinful people and warning of how awful it would be if armies of men instead of grasshoppers invaded the land of Israel. God wanted His people to listen to the warning so He could save and bless them.

....

*Dear God, thank You for the book of Joel. Help me
as I read it and keep coming back to it in the future.
Teach me what You want me to learn from it to apply
to my life and to share with others. Amen.*

A BIG, GOOD GOAL

*I will set no sinful thing
in front of my eyes.*
PSALM 101:3

Psalm 101:3 is a big promise to make and a difficult one to keep these days. With phones and Wi-Fi devices right in our pockets, we have many opportunities to put sinful things in front of our eyes. So it's extra wise to make this verse our goal. It means being super careful about what we read and watch and look at to make sure those things don't lead us to go against God's Word and into things that are full of harm and trouble. With God's constant help, we can rise to the challenge to make setting no sinful thing in front of our eyes our goal. We can ask Him to fill us with wisdom to choose and use the internet and social media in good ways instead of sinful ways. And if we do mess up, then we confess to God right away and ask for help from others in our life who want to help us keep away from sin too.

....

*Dear God, please give me the wisdom I need to help
me keep away from watching and reading sinful things.
I want to obey You in this because I know You want to
protect me from things that might seem like no big deal
at first but can actually be really harmful to me. Amen.*

WHAT YOU LISTEN TO, SAY, AND DO

*Let the teaching of Christ and His words keep on living in you.
These make your lives rich and full of wisdom.*
COLOSSIANS 3:16

We all need wisdom, not just for what we watch and look at, but for choosing what we listen to and say and do as well. Everything that we put into our minds through our eyes and ears affects what we say and do. So this scripture in Colossians 3 helps guide us. If we let all the teachings of Jesus and His words actively live in us—meaning we focus on, listen to, and obey them most of all as we try our best to live like Jesus did—we will have lives that are rich and full of wisdom. ("Rich" in this case doesn't necessarily mean a life full of lots of money, but it means a life full of all the goodness God wants to give us—especially the things money can never buy.) So even as you do something as simple as choosing your favorite music, you can ask yourself, *Does this help me to focus on God and following Jesus or not? If not, what could I choose instead that would help me focus on Him?*

....

*Dear God, please help me to make even the smallest choices
in my life with wisdom from You. Please help me to strive
to do and say all things in ways that honor You! Amen.*

WISDOM FOR WHAT YOU SAY, PART 1

We make a horse go wherever we want it to go by a small bit in its mouth. We turn its whole body by this. Sailing ships are driven by strong winds. But a small rudder turns a large ship whatever way the man at the wheel wants the ship to go. The tongue is also a small part of the body, but it can speak big things. See how a very small fire can set many trees on fire. The tongue is a fire.

JAMES 3:3–6

I love remembering when Jodi and Lilly first started talking! Ask your parents what your first words were and see if they have any videos of them. When a baby starts talking, it's a big deal. And what we say never stops being a big deal. The Bible is clear about how powerful the words we say are, so we need to remember God's wisdom that we should be careful with them. Proverbs 21:23 says, "He who watches over his mouth and his tongue keeps his soul from troubles." And Ephesians 4:29 says, "Watch your talk! No bad words should be coming from your mouth. Say what is good. Your words should help others grow as Christians."

Dear God, please help me to remember that the words I say matter and they are powerful. Please help me to use my mouth wisely. Amen.

WISDOM FOR WHAT YOU SAY, PART 2

*If a person thinks he is religious, but does
not keep his tongue from speaking bad things,
he is fooling himself. His religion is worth nothing.*
JAMES 1:26

If we say we love and believe in and follow Jesus as our Savior, then we need to care about what we are saying and the impact our words have. And if we mess up and say bad things or lies, we need to confess and correct that sin as quickly as possible. Here are more scriptures that help us remember how powerful our mouths and tongues are:

- "A gentle answer turns away anger, but a sharp word causes anger. The tongue of the wise uses much learning in a good way, but the mouth of fools speaks in a foolish way" (Proverbs 15:1–2).

- "The one who talks much will for sure sin, but he who is careful what he says is wise" (Proverbs 10:19).

- "If you want joy in your life and have happy days, keep your tongue from saying bad things and your lips from talking bad about others. Turn away from what is sinful. Do what is good. Look for peace and go after it. The Lord watches over those who are right with Him. He hears their prayers. But the Lord is against those who sin" (1 Peter 3:10–12).

Dear God, like Psalm 141:3 says, please "put a watch over my mouth. Keep watch over the door of my lips." Thank You! Amen.

Matching Words and Actions

But to sinful people nothing is pure. Both their minds and their hearts are bad. They say they know God, but by the way they act, they show that they do not. They are sinful people. They will not obey and are of no use for any good work.
TITUS 1:15–16

Our words matter, and so do our actions. If we say all the right things but then we don't do what is right, our words mean nothing and we become a hypocrite—a person who says one thing but does the opposite. Maybe you've experienced someone like that at school—someone who says the right things to look good for the teacher, but behind the teacher's back that person is always breaking the rules or doing mean things. Hypocrites are dishonest and cannot be trusted, and we should never want to be like them. This scripture in Titus talks about people who say they know God but their actions don't match up with that. We should always strive to make sure that what we say about loving and believing in God and following Jesus matches up with how we live our lives.

Dear God, please help me not just to say that I love and follow You but to show others that is true by what I do. Amen.

WISDOM FROM THE
BOOK OF AMOS

The Lord says to the people of Israel,
"Look for Me and live."
AMOS 5:4

Amos was a shepherd and a fruit picker, just a totally ordinary kind of guy who became a prophet for God. This reminds us that God can use anyone He chooses, no matter their background, to do His good works. Amos warned his people that even though things were going well for them overall, they would soon be judged for their sin they were holding on to. There are good lessons for us in the book of Amos to remind us that we should look for any sin we're holding on to underneath the good in our lives and confess that sin to God and ask for forgiveness. God loves to forgive and bless us when we turn back to Him.

Dear God, thank You for the book of Amos. Help me
as I read it and keep coming back to it in the future.
Teach me what You want me to learn from it to apply
to my life and to share with others. Amen.

WISDOM FROM THE BOOK OF OBADIAH

"For the day of the Lord is near for all nations. As you have done, it will be done to you. What you do will come back to you on your own head."
OBADIAH 1:15

The book of Obadiah has only twenty-one verses total! That's the shortest book in the Old Testament. In it, God's prophet Obadiah had a message for Edom, a not-so-nice neighbor nation of Israel. Edom would be destroyed because of how they celebrated when bad things happened to Israel and how they fought against Israel when they needed Edom's help. The book of Obadiah helps show us how protective God is of His people, and He wants to bring justice to those who mistreat them.

Dear God, thank You for the book of Obadiah. Help me as I read it and keep coming back to it in the future. Teach me what You want me to learn from it to apply to my life and to share with others. Amen.

WISDOM ABOUT PEER PRESSURE

Do not want to be like those who do wrong. . . .
Trust in the Lord, and do good. So you will live
in the land and will be fed. Be happy in the Lord.
And He will give you the desires of your heart.
PSALM 37:1, 3–4

It's not always easy to stay away from those who do wrong.
Sometimes it seems fun and harmless to be like them and just
go along with whatever seems popular, even if deep down
you know that what is popular is wrong. So it takes courage to
stay away from those doing wrong, especially if you're feeling
pressure from people you thought were your friends. But God
promises that if you trust Him and do good, you will have everything you need and He will give you the things that make
you happy because first you are happy in Him!

Dear God, please help me to have wisdom and courage
not to want to be like those who do wrong. I want to do
what is wise and makes You happy. I trust that's the
best way for me to be happy too. Amen.

WISDOM FROM THE BOOK OF JONAH

*The Word of the Lord came to Jonah the son of Amittai,
saying, "Get up and go to the large city of Nineveh,
and preach against it. For their sin has come up before Me."
But Jonah ran away from the Lord going toward Tarshish.
He went down to Joppa and found a ship which was going
to Tarshish. Jonah paid money, and got on the ship to
go with them, to get away from the Lord.*

JONAH 1:1–3

Jonah is one of the most well-known names in the Bible because of his time spent inside the belly of a big fish! What an incredible story that is! Jonah ended up inside that fish because he did not want to go be God's prophet in Nineveh—and so he disobeyed. We can learn much wisdom from Jonah's story, especially that even if He must take extreme measures, God will show us what we've done wrong and help us to get back on the path He has planned for us.

*Dear God, thank You for the book of Jonah. Help me
as I read it and keep coming back to it in the future.
Teach me what You want me to learn from it to apply
to my life and to share with others. Amen.*

WISDOM FROM THE BOOK OF MICAH

What should I bring to the Lord when I bow down before the God on high? Should I come to Him with burnt gifts, with calves a year old? Will the Lord be pleased with thousands of rams, or with 10,000 rivers of oil? Should I give my first-born to pay for not obeying? Should I give the fruit of my body for the sin of my soul? O man, He has told you what is good. What does the Lord ask of you but to do what is fair and to love kindness, and to walk without pride with your God?

MICAH 6:6–8

The nations of Judah and Israel were worshipping idols instead of God and were mistreating poor and needy people. Through the prophet Micah, God warned them that they would be destroyed for their bad behavior. Micah preached a message from God of both judgment and mercy, showing that God hates sin but never hates the people who sin. He wants each person to confess their sin, turn away from it, and turn back to Him for forgiveness and love. He wants us to honor Him with the ways we act fairly and kindly and humbly in our lives.

Dear God, thank You for the book of Micah. Help me as I read it and keep coming back to it in the future. Teach me what You want me to learn from it to apply to my life and to share with others. Amen.

WISDOM ABOUT SHARING THE GOOD NEWS

*I am not ashamed of the Good News. It is the power of God.
It is the way He saves men from the punishment of their sins if
they put their trust in Him. It is for the Jew first and for all other
people also. The Good News tells us we are made right with God
by faith in Him. Then, by faith we live that new life through Him.
The Holy Writings say, "A man right with God lives by faith."*
ROMANS 1:16–17

Even the wisest people have things here and there that they
get embarrassed by or ashamed of. But no Christian should
ever feel embarrassed or ashamed of Jesus. As the apostle
Paul shared in Romans 1, we should all want to be able to say
this—that we are not ashamed of the Good News that Jesus
came to earth to live a perfect life and teach us, then died
on the cross to pay for our sins, and then rose to life again
and offers us eternal life too. When we share this Good News
with others, we help spread God's power to save people from
their sins.

*Dear God, please give me the wisdom I need never to be
ashamed to share the Good News about Jesus! Thank You
for loving all people and wanting to save us from sin! Amen.*

WISDOM IN THE
HARD THINGS

*When someone does something bad to you, do not do the
same thing to him. When someone talks about you, do not talk
about him. Instead, pray that good will come to him. You were
called to do this so you might receive good things from God.*
1 PETER 3:9

Even though being mistreated feels awful, you can choose to
learn wisdom from the experience. You can learn good lessons
when someone is mean or rude or does bad things to you—you
can learn what *not* to do to someone else. You can learn to
choose better or "take the high road." God wants us to take
that higher road and not get revenge on others who mistreat
us. In fact, He wants us to instead pray that good things will
come to the people who do bad to us. That's sure not easy,
but remember that God wants to bless you when you obey His
wisdom on this. Ask Him to help you, and then see how He
rewards you!

....

*Dear God, I pray for those who treat me badly. Please help them
to stop doing bad things and instead know You as Savior and
want to share Your love. Please bless them with good things to
fill their lives. Help me not to want to get revenge. Instead,
help me to trust in You to take care of everything. Amen.*

WISDOM FROM THE BOOK OF NAHUM

The Lord is good, a safe place in times of trouble. And He knows those who come to Him to be safe. But He will put an end to Nineveh by making a flood flow over it. And He will drive those who hate Him into darkness.

NAHUM 1:7–8

Remember when God sent Jonah to preach to the people of Nineveh? (And Jonah finally made it there after spending a few days inside the big fish for disobeying at first!) The people of Nineveh did repent, and God had mercy on them, but one hundred years later they were back to doing bad things like they were in trouble for the first time! So God sent a message through the prophet Nahum that God was going to destroy Nineveh, and He did just that about fifty years after Nahum warned them. The book is a lesson that we must remember what a good, safe place God is for all who trust and follow Him. But He will destroy those who hate Him.

....

Dear God, thank You for the book of Nahum. Help me as I read it and keep coming back to it in the future. Teach me what You want me to learn from it to apply to my life and to share with others. Amen.

WISDOM ABOUT YOUR IDENTITY

*And God made man in His own likeness. In the likeness
of God He made him. He made both male and female.*
GENESIS 1:27

You might hear a lot these days about people trying to figure out their identity. If we look to God, that's where we find it! His Word is clear in Genesis 1 that God made us in His likeness. He has made boys and girls to grow up into men and women, and He has given us the Bible to guide us in how to live and love like He does. Here are more scriptures that help us have wisdom to know our identity is in God and we become new creations in Jesus when we accept Him as Savior.

- "Christ lives in me. The life I now live in this body, I live by putting my trust in the Son of God. He was the One Who loved me and gave Himself for me" (Galatians 2:20).

- "But you are a chosen group of people. You are the King's religious leaders. You are a holy nation. You belong to God. He has done this for you so you can tell others how God has called you out of darkness into His great light" (1 Peter 2:9).

*Dear God, please help me always to have wisdom that
my identity is found in You! Thank You for creating me
and saving me from sin! I live my life with trust in You,
following Jesus Christ, who lives in me! Amen.*

WISDOM ABOUT BEING PROUD

If anyone wants to be proud, he should be proud of what the Lord has done. It is not what a man thinks and says of himself that is important. It is what God thinks of him.
2 CORINTHIANS 10:17–18

Of course you feel happy when you accomplish something cool, right? And that's great! Just don't forget to give God credit for each good and cool thing you do. That's a great way to stay humble and never become full of pride in yourself rather than in God. He deserves every bit of praise and worship because He is the One who gives you your gifts and abilities.

Dear God, I want to be way prouder of You than I am of anything cool I do. You are the One who gives me my talents and abilities. Please help me to use them well in the ways You want me to, especially to share Your love and truth with others. Amen.

WISDOM FROM THE BOOK OF HABAKKUK

*Even if the fig tree does not grow figs and there is no
fruit on the vines, even if the olives do not grow and
the fields give no food, even if there are no sheep within
the fence and no cattle in the cattle-building, yet I will
have joy in the Lord. I will be glad in the God Who saves me.*
HABAKKUK 3:17–18

Habakkuk was a prophet of God who had lots of questions. He started out by writing, "O Lord, how long must I call for help before You will hear? I cry out to You, 'We are being hurt!' But You do not save us" (Habakkuk 1:2). We all can relate to asking God questions. We sometimes wonder why we must wait so long on Him or why He doesn't answer our prayers the way we want Him to. We can learn from Habakkuk that even though this prophet never got the exact answers he was hoping for from God, he got answers that reminded him of this: God is all powerful and all good, and He will work out His perfect plans in His perfect timing. We must always trust what Habakkuk learned in our own lives today too.

*Dear God, thank You for the book of Habakkuk.
Help me as I read it and keep coming back to it in
the future. Teach me what You want me to learn from
it to apply to my life and to share with others. Amen.*

A Parable About Prayer

*Jesus. . .said, "There was a man in one of the cities who
was head of the court. His work was to say if a person was
guilty or not. This man was not afraid of God. He did not
respect any man. In that city there was a woman whose
husband had died. She kept coming to him and saying,
'Help me! There is someone who is working against me.' For
awhile he would not help her. Then he began to think, '. . . I will
see that this woman whose husband has died gets her rights
because I get tired of her coming all the time.' " Then the Lord
said, "Listen to the words of the sinful man who is head of the
court. Will not God make the things that are right come to His
chosen people who cry day and night to Him? Will He wait a
long time to help them? . . . He will be quick to help them."*

Luke 18:1–8

Sometimes we feel like giving up when it seems like God isn't
hearing us or is taking too long to answer. This picture-story
from Jesus reminds us that we should "always pray and not
give up." That is wonderful wisdom from Jesus that we should
never, ever forget!

*Dear Jesus, thank You that You taught me never
to give up on prayer. Please help me when I do feel
like giving up. Remind me of this story. Amen.*

WISDOM FROM GREAT
FAITH HEROES

*Faith makes us sure of what we hope for and
gives us proof of what we cannot see. It was their
faith that made our ancestors pleasing to God.*
HEBREWS 11:1–2 CEV

We can get a lot of wisdom from the lives of people with
great faith who have gone before us. Hebrews 11 is a wonderful chapter of the Bible to help us remember a whole list of
great faith heroes, people like Noah and Moses and Joseph
and Sarah and Rahab, who continued to believe in God and
His promises, even during the most difficult times. Like them,
we should want to hold on to our faith, no matter what. Think
about the people among your family and friends who have
super strong faith in God, those who are still living and those
who have passed away. Keep looking up to and honoring them
and their example, now and every day of your life too!

*Dear God, please help me to remember everyone who
has gone before me who kept great faith in You.
I want to be so strong in my faith too. Amen.*

WISDOM ABOUT EQUALITY

You are now children of God because you have put your trust in Christ Jesus. All of you who have been baptized to show you belong to Christ have become like Christ. God does not see you as a Jew or as a Greek. He does not see you as a servant or as a person free to work. He does not see you as a man or as a woman. You are all one in Christ.
GALATIANS 3:26–28

You might hear the word *equality* a lot these days, and it's so important to have wisdom about who alone gives real equality—Jesus! Because of sin in the world, people will never get equality exactly right. There will always be bad people trying to say some groups of people are better than others. But don't ever listen to or join them. In God's eyes, because of Jesus, every single person is the same in value. We all matter so much to God that He sent Jesus to die to save us from our sins. And when anyone trusts in Jesus, they become a child of the one true God, the King of all kings. That makes us all equally royal, and we should want to share that awesome truth with everyone we can!

....

Dear God, You offer the only true equality through Jesus. Thank You that anyone can be Your child by trusting that only Jesus saves. Help me to share Your love and truth and wisdom. Amen.

WISDOM FROM THE BOOK OF ZEPHANIAH

"Do not let your hands lose their strength. The Lord your God is with you, a Powerful One Who wins the battle. He will have much joy over you. With His love He will give you new life. He will have joy over you with loud singing."
ZEPHANIAH 3:16–17

The prophet Zephaniah preached a scary message from God in the first chapter of his book about awful suffering and judgment for the nation of Judah and all nations who turn away from God. Then he begged the people to turn to God before it was too late. And in the last chapter, he preached that despite all the bad things that will happen to those who reject God, there is great hope in God's promises for all who love and trust and obey Him.

Dear God, thank You for the book of Zephaniah. Help me as I read it and keep coming back to it in the future. Teach me what You want me to learn from it to apply to my life and to share with others. Amen.

WISDOM WHEN YOUR HEART IS BROKEN, PART 1

Jesus said. . . "In the world you will have much trouble.
But take hope! I have power over the world!"
JOHN 16:31, 33

~~~~~

We wish it were true that our hearts would never break in this world, but sadly it's not. Awful things do happen to every single one of us. Loved ones die, parents get divorced, friends betray us. Houses burn down, favorite things get stolen. People get sick or injured. Friends and loved ones move far away. And even lesser things can make us feel heartbroken. In any of those situations, we have a very important choice to make about our relationship with God—do we get closer to Him or further away? Do we choose to let Him help and comfort us, or do we choose anger and blame God? The wise choice is to grow closer to God. Psalm 34:17–18 says, "Those who are right with the Lord cry, and He hears them. And He takes them from all their troubles. The Lord is near to those who have a broken heart."

....

Dear God, please help me to choose wisely when my
heart feels broken. Help me not to turn away from You
in anger and blame. Help me to remember that You are
near and You want to heal my broken heart. Amen.

WISDOM WHEN YOUR HEART IS BROKEN, PART 2

Praise the Lord! For it is good to sing praises to our God. . . .
He heals those who have a broken heart.
PSALM 147:1, 3

If you have a broken bone, you shouldn't run away screaming and angry from the doctors and nurses who can fix it. How silly, right? You might *wish* you could run away, because the process of fixing it is painful and scary and feels like it takes forever. But worse would be never fixing the broken bone at all. It's the same way with a broken heart. God is the only One who can truly heal it. Wisely choosing to get closer to Him even when your heart feels broken doesn't mean you instantly feel all better. You will still hurt for a long time and might feel all kinds of emotions, including anger and fear. But if you let God, He will comfort you and help you with those emotions. It does take time to heal your broken heart though, just like a broken bone takes time to heal. Keep praying to God. Keep reading His Word. Keep going to church and letting other people who love God encourage you. God will show you His love and care in many different ways as He heals you.

....

Dear God, please help me to be patient
as I let You comfort me and show me
Your love in all kinds of ways. Amen.

WISDOM WHEN YOUR HEART IS BROKEN, PART 3

I pray that you will be able to understand how wide and how long and how high and how deep His love is. I pray that you will know the love of Christ. His love goes beyond anything we can understand. I pray that you will be filled with God Himself.
EPHESIANS 3:18–19

When your heart feels broken from losing a loved one and you're choosing to get closer to God, it's wise to write in a journal to keep track of how you see God helping you. You might wish so much that He would bring back the loved one who died, but if you keep track, you will see how God is bringing love to you in other ways, through other people. If you write down the many memories you have of a loved one you have lost, you can focus on being thankful for all the love and time you did have together. And if your loved one knew Jesus as their Savior and you do too, you can write down all the things you want to tell them and do with them when you spend forever together in perfect heaven with God.

....

Dear God, please help me to keep track of all the ways You help me heal and show me Your awesome love when my heart is broken. I don't want to forget how well You take care of me. Amen.

WISDOM FROM THE BOOK OF HAGGAI

" 'Be strong, all you people of the land,' says the Lord.
'Do the work, for I am with you,' says the Lord of All.
'As I promised you when you came out of Egypt,
My Spirit is with you. Do not be afraid.' "
HAGGAI 2:4–5

The prophet Haggai had a message for God's people to get back to work rebuilding the temple in Jerusalem. At first they had a good plan and a good start, but then they got distracted and let the project sit for years. We do that kind of thing sometimes too, don't we? We get excited about good things God has asked us to do, and we enjoy them for a while, and then we get off track to do our own thing instead. The book of Haggai can be a great reminder to us to keep asking God what He wants us to do and then never give up on His good plans for us! If we do get off track, God is happy to help us get right back to good work.

....

Dear God, thank You for the book of Haggai. Help me
as I read it and keep coming back to it in the future.
Teach me what You want me to learn from it to apply
to my life and to share with others. Amen.

WISDOM FROM THE BOOK OF ZECHARIAH

"The Lord of All says, 'I am going to save My people from the land of the east and from the land of the west. I will bring them back and they will live in Jerusalem. They will be My people and I will be their God. I will be faithful and do what is right and good for them.'"
ZECHARIAH 8:7–8

Like Haggai, the prophet Zechariah also preached to the people of Judah to encourage them to finish the good work they had started of rebuilding the temple in Jerusalem. He told them it would one day be the home of the Messiah Himself (the Savior they were hoping for, whom we know is Jesus Christ)! Zechariah kept encouraging the people and told them about all the blessings that would come to the Jewish people once they had obeyed and finished their good work. We can read Zechariah's words and let them inspire and motivate us to do the good work God has for us too. When we do, we will be blessed, and we have already been so very blessed by the gift of Jesus Christ as our Savior from sin.

....

Dear God, thank You for the book of Zechariah. Help me as I read it and keep coming back to it in the future. Teach me what You want me to learn from it to apply to my life and to share with others. Amen.

WISDOM WHEN WE MAKE BAD CHOICES, PART 1

*And Jesus said, "There was a man who had two sons.
The younger son said to his father, 'Father, let me have the
part of the family riches that will be coming to me.' Then the
father divided all that he owned between his two sons. Soon
after that the younger son took all that had been given to him
and went to another country far away. There he spent all he had
on wild and foolish living. When all his money was spent, he was
hungry. There was no food in the land. He went to work for a
man in this far away country. His work was to feed pigs. He was
so hungry he was ready to eat the outside part of the ears of
the corn the pigs ate because no one gave him anything.
He began to think about what he had done."*

LUKE 15:11–17

In this parable, Jesus was teaching about God's great love for
us, even when we make bad choices, just like the younger son
in this story. If you've ever made bad choices, God wants you
to think about what you've done and pray to Him about them.

*Dear God, please help me to think about my choices
and admit to You when I've sinned against You.
Please forgive me and help me not to make the
same bad choices again in the future. Amen.*

WISDOM WHEN WE MAKE BAD CHOICES, PART 2

*"I will get up and go to my father. I will say to him,
'Father, I have sinned against heaven and against you.'"*
LUKE 15:18

The parable from Jesus continues: "The son got up and went to his father. While he was yet a long way off, his father saw him. The father was full of loving-pity for him. He ran and threw his arms around him and kissed him. The son said to him, 'Father, I have sinned against heaven and against you. I am not good enough to be called your son.' But the father said to the workmen he owned, 'Hurry! Get the best coat and put it on him. Put a ring on his hand and shoes on his feet. Bring the calf that is fat and kill it. Let us eat and be glad. For my son was dead and now he is alive again. He was lost and now he is found. Let us eat and have a good time'" (Luke 15:20–24).

God loves us just like the father in the story loved his sons. He does not want to hold our sins against us. When we confess them to Him and come back to close relationship with Him, He feels like throwing us a big party too!

....

*Dear God, thank You so much for Your
amazing grace to forgive my sins. Thank You
for celebrating me and loving me so much! Amen.*

WISDOM WHEN SCHOOLWORK IS HARD

You should be happy when you have all kinds of tests. You know these prove your faith. It helps you not to give up. Learn well how to wait so you will be strong and complete and in need of nothing. If you do not have wisdom, ask God for it.
JAMES 1:2–5

Have you ever struggled with a particular subject in school? Maybe when you were first learning fractions in math or different types of sentences in language arts? Life can feel so stressful when you're just not "getting it." In those times, pray for wisdom. Ask God to help you to continue to do your best and try your hardest while also being patient with yourself. Keep studying and practicing, and God might suddenly help you make the connections in your brain. Or He will lead you to the right tutor or friend who knows how to explain things in just the right way. The most important thing is not to give up. You might not understand *yet*, but eventually, with God's help, you will!

Dear God, please give me wisdom and understanding as I try to learn new and hard things. Help me not to give up until I've "got it"! Amen.

WISDOM TO
REMEMBER WHEN

Moses said to the people, "Remember this day in
which you went out of Egypt, out of the land where
you were made to stay and work. For the Lord
brought you out of this place by a powerful hand."
EXODUS 13:3

Sometimes we want to forget the bad things that have happened to us because they were awful and we're so glad they're over. But doing that isn't always wise. We do need to remember them in some ways so that we never forget how God helped us through them. Looking back and remembering grows our faith and helps us trust that God will always rescue us again in the future. Moses told the people of Israel to remember the amazing day that God finally brought them out of slavery in Egypt. Just as they did, we need to remember all the amazing ways God has delivered us from hard things too.

Dear God, every bit of help and rescue I have ever received
ultimately comes from You, through so many ways and
so many people! I don't ever want to forget, and I trust
You to help and rescue me again and again! Amen.

WISDOM FROM THE BOOK OF MALACHI

*The names of those who worshiped the Lord and
honored Him were written down before Him in a
Book to be remembered. "They will be Mine says the
Lord of All, on that day that I gather My special people."*
MALACHI 3:16–17

Malachi was a prophet of God who spoke a message to help bring God's people back into close relationship with Him. God wants that for us too. He is upset when we choose sin that hurts our relationship with Him, and He wants us to confess and turn away from it so that we can be close with Him again. You know what that's like in your own friendships. If you make a bad choice and hurt a friend's feelings, the conflict you have caused makes it seem like you aren't good friends at all. But when you ask forgiveness and your friend forgives you, then you can get back to being BFFs again! Malachi wanted to help God's people—and that includes you—to be even closer than great BFFs with God!

*Dear God, thank You for the book of Malachi. Help me
as I read it and keep coming back to it in the future.
Teach me what You want me to learn from it to apply
to my life and to share with others. Amen.*

Be Ready For Good Work

In a big house there are not only things made of gold
and silver, but also of wood and clay. Some are of more use
than others. Some are used every day. If a man lives a clean
life, he will be like a dish made of gold. He will be respected
and set apart for good use by the owner of the house. Turn
away from the sinful things young people want to do. Go after
what is right. Have a desire for faith and love and peace.
Do this with those who pray to God from a clean heart.
2 TIMOTHY 2:20–22

This scripture helps you think about how you want God to use
your life. Do you want to be just like regular everyday wood
and clay, or do you want to be like shining gold used for the
coolest purposes? With wisdom to live a clean life, as far away
from sin as possible, God can use you for the very best things
He has planned.

....

Dear God, please constantly show me what areas
of my life need to be cleaned up. Help me to stay far
away from things that are bad for me. I want You to
use me in the wonderful ways You created me for. Amen.

WISDOM FROM CREATION

Men know about God. He has made it plain to them.
Men cannot say they do not know about God. From the
beginning of the world, men could see what God is like
through the things He has made. This shows His power
that lasts forever. It shows that He is God.
ROMANS 1:19–20

What are your favorite things about nature and science? My girls and I especially love spending time at the ocean and studying the sky at night. Do you know that we gain wisdom simply by looking around and appreciating nature and science and the whole beautiful world God created? God has shown Himself through everything He has made in creation. So no person can say they know nothing about God. Anyone can know that He is real by the tiny details of a pretty flower or in the highest peaks of a rocky mountain range. Anyone can see Him in the intricate ways our human bodies are designed and in the ways animals know how to hunt for their food or build themselves a home. Our creator God is awesome, and He deserves all of our worship and praise!

Dear God, I love looking at Your work in all
the things You have made. Thank You for making
Yourself known through Your amazing creation! Amen.

WISDOM FROM THE BOOK OF MATTHEW

He said to them, "But who do you say that I am?"
Simon Peter said, "You are the Christ, the Son of the
living God." Jesus said to him, "Simon, son of Jonah,
you are happy because you did not learn this from
man. My Father in heaven has shown you this."
MATTHEW 16:15–17

The book of Matthew is the first book of the New Testament in the Bible. Four hundred years passed from the time between the last book in the Old Testament, Malachi, until the time of the book of Matthew. It's one of the four Gospels—books that tell about the arrival and life and ministry of Jesus Christ. He's the star because He was (and is!) the Messiah, which means "chosen one," whom the Jewish people were eagerly waiting for. He had been promised by the prophets of God. Jesus said, "Do not think that I have come to do away with the Law of Moses or the writings of the early preachers. I have not come to do away with them but to complete them" (Matthew 5:17).

Dear God, thank You for the book of Matthew.
Help me as I read it and keep coming back to it in
the future. Teach me what You want me to learn from
it to apply to my life and to share with others. Amen.

WISDOM ABOUT GOD'S PROTECTION

At my first trial no one helped me. Everyone left me. I hope this will not be held against them. But the Lord was with me. He gave me power to preach the Good News so all the people who do not know God might hear. I was taken from the mouth of the lion. The Lord will look after me and will keep me from every sinful plan they have. He will bring me safe into His holy nation of heaven. May He have all the shining-greatness forever.

2 TIMOTHY 4:16–18

Maybe you've had times when you felt alone with no one to help you or protect you. In those times, you can read and re-member these words that Paul wrote in the Bible. Even with no one else there to help, God Himself was with Paul and pro-tected him and gave him power. And Paul trusted that God would keep away every bad plan that people might have against him. Paul also knew that no matter what happened on earth, God would someday bring him into heaven forever. Paul wrote this in his letter to Timothy to give him wisdom about God's protection, but all of it is true for you to trust today.

Dear God, thank You for Your protection. I trust that no matter what happens here in this world, You will ultimately always keep me safe, because someday You are going to bring me into perfect paradise in heaven with You! Amen.

WISDOM ABOUT STUFF

*"Do not gather together for yourself riches of this earth.
They will be eaten by bugs and become rusted. Men can
break in and steal them. Gather together riches in heaven
where they will not be eaten by bugs or become rusted.
Men cannot break in and steal them. For wherever
your riches are, your heart will be there also."*
MATTHEW 6:19–21

We're always needing to sort through and get rid of stuff in our house—the things we have that seem to pile up quickly, the things we buy that we don't really need, but want for fun. Maybe you have a big collection of toys or stuffed animals or games or movies or extra clothes. Or maybe you wish you did. Whatever the case, we all need wisdom about this. Jesus taught us to be careful because we should be storing up riches for ourselves in heaven, not on earth. We can't take any of our stuff from earth to heaven with us, so we shouldn't get too caught up in having it here on earth. And what does it mean to gather riches in heaven? It means that God will be rewarding us with blessings that last forever there based on the good things we are doing to bring praise to Him here on earth.

*Dear God, please help me to have lots of wisdom about
stuff. Help me to want treasure in heaven much more
than any collection of treasures here on earth. Amen.*

WISDOM FROM THE BOOK OF MARK

*"He came to care for others. He came to
give His life so that many could be bought
by His blood and be made free from sin."*
MARK 10:45

Mark wrote the shortest of the four Gospels that tell about the life and ministry of Jesus. There are similarities and differences between all four of the Gospels because they are written by four different authors with four different personalities and perspectives. (If you and three friends wrote about the same topic, none of you would write it in exactly the same way, right? And that's a good thing! We learn more when multiple authors write about the same thing!) But the Gospels are similar in all the ways that matter most to tell us about the teaching and miracles and death and resurrection of Jesus and how He fulfilled what the prophets had preached in the Old Testament.

*Dear God, thank You for the book of Mark. Help me
as I read it and keep coming back to it in the future.
Teach me what You want me to learn from it to apply
to my life and to share with others. Amen.*

WISDOM TO WANT GOOD CHARACTER

A good name is to be chosen instead of many riches.
Favor is better than silver and gold. The rich and the
poor meet together. The Lord is the maker of them all.
A wise man sees sin and hides himself, but the foolish go on,
and are punished for it. The reward for not having pride
and having the fear of the Lord is riches, honor and life.
PROVERBS 22:1–4

A good name means a good reputation and good character, and it takes wisdom to want that for yourself. When people hear your name, do you want them to think of you in good ways or bad ways? Do you want to be known for things like laziness or lying or rudeness or getting into trouble? Or do you want to be known for things like doing your best and being honest, fair, kind, and worthy of respect? Choose now while you are young to do your very best to have excellent character your whole life. It doesn't mean you will always be perfect, but it means you will live for God and obey His ways of love and fairness and honesty—and you will quickly want to make things right when you make a mistake and do wrong.

Dear God, I want to be known for good character and
a good name because I obey You. Please give me wisdom
and keep me on the right paths following You. Amen.

WISDOM FROM THE BOOK OF LUKE

Many people have written about the things that have happened among us. Those who saw everything. . .and helped teach the Good News have passed these things on to us. . . . I have decided it would be good to write them to you one after the other the way they happened. Then you can be sure you know the truth about the things you have been taught.

LUKE 1:1–4

The Gospel that Luke wrote tells us the most about Jesus' parents and His birth and childhood. It gives us the most detail for our Christmas celebrations of Jesus. Luke wrote to show how Jesus was both human like us but also fully God and totally perfect without sin. Jesus was the only One who could pay the price of sin for us by dying on the cross. And because He took our sin on Himself, He made a way for us to have a good relationship with God. Luke wanted to make sure that everyone reading his Gospel understood that any person at all, no matter who they are or where they come from, could accept Jesus Christ as Savior and have a relationship with God and forever life in heaven.

Dear God, thank You for the book of Luke. Help me as I read it and keep coming back to it in the future. Teach me what You want me to learn from it to apply to my life and to share with others. Amen.

WISDOM ABOUT WORSHIP

Call out with joy to the Lord, all the earth. Be glad as you serve the Lord. Come before Him with songs of joy. Know that the Lord is God. It is He Who made us, and not we ourselves. We are His people and the sheep of His field. Go into His gates giving thanks and into His holy place with praise. Give thanks to Him. Honor His name. For the Lord is good. His loving-kindness lasts forever. And He is faithful to all people and to all their children-to-come.
PSALM 100

Do you have favorite worship songs you love to sing at church? We hope you sing them all throughout the week too! Sometimes we forget how important it is to sing to God every day, but the psalms are so good to remind us. When we sing praise songs to God, we put our focus where it needs to be— on God!—with beautiful music and words reminding us of His awesome character and love and power.

Dear God, please help me to remember to sing to You every day, no matter what I'm going through. I know songs of praise to You can fill me with joy and peace because of focusing on how awesome You are and how much You love me. Amen.

WISDOM FROM THE
BOOK OF JOHN

These are written so you may believe that Jesus is the Christ,
the Son of God. When you put your trust in Him, you will
have life that lasts forever through His name.
JOHN 20:31

The book of John is the last of the four Gospels about the life
and ministry of Jesus. The book of John doesn't give any detail
at all about Jesus' life as a child, but it focuses a lot on the final
days of Jesus' life on earth. Over half of the book is about the
events and Jesus' teaching during his last week on earth. Some
of His last earthly words to His disciples were "Do not let your
heart be troubled. You have put your trust in God, put your
trust in Me also. There are many rooms in My Father's house.
If it were not so, I would have told you. I am going away to
make a place for you. After I go and make a place for you, I will
come back and take you with Me" (John 14:1–3). These words
are meant to encourage us today too!

Dear God, thank You for the book of John. Help me
as I read it and keep coming back to it in the future.
Teach me what You want me to learn from it to apply
to my life and to share with others. Amen.

REST WELL, PART 1

On the seventh day God ended His work which
He had done. And He rested on the seventh day
from all His work which He had done. Then God
honored the seventh day and made it holy, because
in it He rested from all His work which He had done.
GENESIS 2:2–3

You might feel annoyed by your parents setting bedtimes and always trying to make sure you get enough sleep. *What's the big deal?* you might think. But getting enough rest really is a big deal. God thought it was such a big deal, He set aside an entire day of the week for it! So you should actually feel super grateful to God and to your parents for caring so much about you that they want you to rest. It's good for your physical health in many ways, and it's good for your spiritual health too. God intends rest for both actual sleeping and for time simply spent with Him, relaxing while you focus on how great He is and how much He loves you!

Dear God, please help me to be thankful for rest
time rather than annoyed by it. You designed it,
and it's so good for me. Thank You! Amen.

REST WeLL, ParT 2

"Come to Me, all of you who work and have heavy loads. I will give you rest. Follow My teachings and learn from Me. I am gentle and do not have pride. You will have rest for your souls. For My way of carrying a load is easy and My load is not heavy."
MATTHEW 11:28–30

Let these scriptures help you learn even more about how important good rest is to God. He doesn't want you to be constantly busy and stressed and exhausted. He wants you to be full of His peace, and for that you need plenty of actual sleep and plenty of time spent learning from Him, worshipping Him, and praying to Him.

- "The followers of Jesus came back to Him. They told Jesus all they had done and taught. He said to them, 'Come away from the people. Be by yourselves and rest' " (Mark 6:30–31).

- "Be quiet and know that I am God. I will be honored among the nations. I will be honored in the earth. The Lord of All is with us. The God of Jacob is our strong place" (Psalm 46:10–11).

Dear God, please help these verses stick in my mind forever, to remind me of how important it is to rest well and especially to rest in You! Amen.

WISDOM FROM THE BOOK OF ACTS

"You will receive power when the Holy Spirit comes into your life. You will tell about Me in the city of Jerusalem and over all the countries of Judea and Samaria and to the ends of the earth."

ACTS 1:8

At the end of the Gospels, Jesus had risen from the dead and appeared to various people to prove that He was alive. The book of Acts picks up right where the Gospel of Luke left off (and is written by the same doctor Luke!) and soon Jesus went up to heaven to be with God the Father. But He didn't want to leave people alone without Him on earth. He promised to send the Holy Spirit in His place. The book of Acts tells about how that promise came true and how the group of believers in Jesus, called the *church*, started out with 120 people and then grew and grew and grew as those believers kept spreading the Good News about our Savior Jesus and more and more people believed in Him.

Dear God, thank You for the book of Acts. Help me as I read it and keep coming back to it in the future. Teach me what You want me to learn from it to apply to my life and to share with others. Amen.

LOOKING UP TO OTHERS, PART 1

The one who says he belongs to Christ
should live the same kind of life Christ lived.
1 JOHN 2:6

Think of your favorite famous people. Are they athletes, actors, artists, and/or musicians? What are all the things you know about them, and why are you their fan? Have you been to their games or concerts or shows? All of that is so fun when we also use wisdom about celebrities as we look up to them. We should never become so obsessed with them to the point we practically worship them. They are never perfect, and we must never forget that. Jesus is the one and only perfect famous person, and He alone should be worshipped. Only He should be the One we try to live like.

. . . .

Dear God, help me to have wisdom about looking
up to famous people. I want Jesus to be my first
and favorite person I look up to. I want to worship
Him alone and live my life like Him. Amen.

LOOKING UP TO OTHERS, PART 2

Follow my way of thinking as I follow Christ.
1 CORINTHIANS 11:1

Far more important than having celebrities you look up to is having mentors you look up to. These are people who have lived longer than you who can help you through the stages of life ahead since they have already been there, done that. Your parents are naturally your mentors, and sometimes a great mentor can be an older sibling or grandparent or cousin or aunt or uncle. Or you can find a mentor among older friends you know through your church or activities or community. They should definitely be people who love and follow Jesus so that they teach you more about loving and following Him too. Odds are, you will never build a relationship with a famous celebrity, but you can definitely build a relationship with great personal mentors who will be far more valuable to you. They can actually be a part of your life to help you learn and grow.

Dear God, please send me the right mentors into my life who love You and who will help teach and guide me to live like Jesus. Thank You! Amen.

Be a Wise Young Leader

*In all things show them how to live by your life and
by right teaching. You should be wise in what you say.
Then the one who is against you will be ashamed and
will not be able to say anything bad about you.*
TITUS 2:7–8

Even while you're young, you can be a leader to others. At school, at church, in your community, and in your activities, there will always be younger kids who look up to you. Ask God to help you find opportunities to lead and mentor them intentionally. Maybe you can be a helper in a Sunday school class or at VBS or in a dance class or with a sports team. And you can simply show the younger kids in your life how much you care about them and want to get to know them. As you build friendships with kids younger than you, you can become a great mentor to them as you keep following Jesus and they look up to and follow you.

*Dear God, as I look up to and follow good and wise leaders
and mentors who love You, help me to be a good leader
and mentor to others too. Show me the people You want
me to help, and grow me in wisdom to lead well. Amen.*

WISDOM FROM THE
BOOK OF ROMANS

*Jesus died for our sins. He was raised from the dead to make
us right with God. Now that we have been made right with
God by putting our trust in Him, we have peace with Him.
It is because of what our Lord Jesus Christ did for us.*
ROMANS 4:25–5:1

The book of Romans is the first in a series of books that are
kind of like reading someone else's mail. You should never do
that without permission, but you absolutely have permission
to read the letters (or *epistles* as they're sometimes called,
which is just a fancy name for letters) included in the Bible.
God wants you to read and learn from them. The book of
Romans was a letter written by the apostle (that's another
fancy word that means a follower of Jesus) Paul. The story of
how his life was totally transformed by Jesus is in Acts. Paul
wrote to the group of believers in the city of Rome to explain
to them fully what it means to have salvation by trusting in
Jesus as the sacrifice for sin.

*Dear God, thank You for the book of Romans. Help me
as I read it and keep coming back to it in the future.
Teach me what You want me to learn from it to apply
to my life and to share with others. Amen.*

WISDOM FOR TOUGH SCHOOL DAYS

Open your heart to teaching,
and your ears to words of much learning.
PROVERBS 23:12

Throughout your school years, you're going to have some teachers who are a lot of fun and easy to learn from, and some who totally aren't. Maybe right now you can think of a particular teacher who is just so hard to be in class with. Maybe his or her rules and assignments seem over-the-top too much and very frustrating. But if the teacher is just strict and tough, you might be able to learn a whole lot if you simply cooperate and show respect. God cares about your situation. Pray for wisdom and ask God to help things get better in class. Let Him show you how to communicate with the teacher well as you do your best in a tough situation.

Dear God, please help me make it through this class
[or this school year] with [name of teacher]. Help me
to do my best and show respect, even when I don't feel
like it. Please help things to get better and make me
stronger and wiser because of this tough situation. Amen.

WISDOM FROM THE BOOKS OF 1 AND 2 CORINTHIANS

This letter is from Paul. I have been chosen by God to be a missionary of Jesus Christ. Sosthenes, a Christian brother, writes also. I write to God's church in the city of Corinth. I write to those who belong to Christ Jesus and to those who are set apart by Him and made holy. I write to all the Christians everywhere who call on the name of Jesus Christ. He is our Lord and their Lord also. May you have loving-favor and peace from God our Father and from the Lord Jesus Christ.

1 Corinthians 1:1–3

The books of 1 and 2 Corinthians are more letters from the apostle Paul, this time to a church in the city of Corinth in Greece. Paul had heard that the Christians in the Corinthian church were not living as they should or treating each other as well as they should. His letters were meant to correct their wrongs and encourage them to do right, according to God's good ways. We can read these letters and let them help us correct our wrongs and do what is right according to God's good ways too!

....

Dear God, thank You for the books of 1 and 2 Corinthians. Help me as I read them and keep coming back to them in the future. Teach me what You want me to learn from them to apply to my life and to share with others. Amen.

WISDOM ABOUT ENDURANCE

*We are pressed on every side, but we still have room
to move. We are often in much trouble, but we never
give up. People make it hard for us, but we are not left
alone. We are knocked down, but we are not destroyed.*
2 CORINTHIANS 4:8–9

Endurance means not to give up but to keep on going even
when things are hard. Think of a time when you've needed great
endurance. Maybe during a sport or activity like cross country
or dance. Or maybe during a really hard test at school when
you felt super stressed and wanted to give up but didn't. The
Bible talks about how we will sometimes have so much trouble in our lives that it feels like we are almost totally defeated.
But God will always help us have just enough new strength and
energy not to give up. He will hold us up and keep us going!

*Dear God, I trust that You keep giving me more
strength and energy and endurance exactly
when I feel like giving up. I never have to give up
when I know You are helping me! Amen.*

WISDOM FROM THE BOOK OF GALATIANS

*Christ made us free. Stay that way. Do not
get chained all over again in the Law
and its kind of religious worship.*
GALATIANS 5:1

Think of the book of Galatians a little bit like the Fourth of July in the United States—a celebration of freedom! Paul wrote this letter to the churches in Galatia to correct them because he was upset that many people there were listening to some false teachers who taught that salvation in Jesus meant to believe in Him plus follow lots of Jewish customs and rules. But that's not true. Salvation in Jesus comes simply from believing in Him and accepting His gift of grace to pay for sin. Unmatched freedom and relief come from trusting that truth and realizing it's Jesus' work of dying on the cross that saves us and gives us eternal life, not any work we do or rules we follow. We should want to share that truth with *all* people so that they can have everlasting freedom in Jesus too!

*Dear God, thank You for the book of Galatians.
Help me as I read it and keep coming back to it in
the future. Teach me what You want me to learn from
it to apply to my life and to share with others. Amen.*

DON'T COMPLAIN

God is helping you obey Him. God is doing what He wants done in you. Be glad you can do the things you should be doing. Do all things without arguing and talking about how you wish you did not have to do them. In that way, you can prove yourselves to be without blame. You are God's children and no one can talk against you, even in a sin-loving and sin-sick world. You are to shine as lights among the sinful people of this world.
PHILIPPIANS 2:13–15

Doing all things without ever arguing or complaining, like the Bible tells us to do, can be super hard. Everyone struggles with this sometimes. So we sure need God's help and wisdom about why it's so good to obey this. If we can keep positive with our words and attitudes as we obey God and follow the plans He has for us, we shine as bright lights to the sinful world around us. And hopefully people who do not trust Jesus as their Savior will want to know more about God's love because they see our lights shining.

. . . .

Dear God, please help me to be a bright light in the darkness of sin around me in this world. I want to shine so brightly that others might know Jesus as Savior too. Amen.

WISDOM FROM THE BOOK OF EPHESIANS

*Let us honor and thank the God and Father of our
Lord Jesus Christ. He has already given us a taste of
what heaven is like. Even before the world was made,
God chose us for Himself because of His love.*

EPHESIANS 1:3–4

The book of Ephesians is Paul's letter to the church in the city
of Ephesus. You can think of it with a big letter *E*, like the first
letter in its name, and the letter *e* in the beginning of the word
encouragement. Because mostly that's what Paul does in this
letter. He is not trying to right a specific wrong in the church
at Ephesus; he simply wants to encourage the believers there
in their faith and identity in Jesus and show them how that
faith and identity should play out in their daily lives. You can
read Ephesians for encouragement in your life too!

....

*Dear God, thank You for the book of Ephesians. Help me
as I read it and keep coming back to it in the future.
Teach me what You want me to learn from it to apply
to my life and to share with others. Amen.*

Be Wise About Confessing Your Sin

*If we say that we have no sin, we lie to ourselves
and the truth is not in us. If we tell Him our sins,
He is faithful and we can depend on Him to forgive
us of our sins. He will make our lives clean from all sin.*

1 John 1:8–9

It's not fun to talk about the bad things we've done, but we need to tell them to God. To pretend like we don't sin is silly, because God knows all about our sins anyway. He sees and knows everything about us, even every single thought we have. So we all must take time to pray and confess and ask forgiveness for our sins rather than try to hide them or act like they're no big deal. A soon as we do confess our sins, God cleans us up and takes the sin as far from us as the east is from the west (Psalm 103:12). That's so awesome! He loves us very much and never wants to hold our sins against us.

Dear God, I confess these sins to You today: [name sins]. And I ask for Your forgiveness. Thank You for being such a forgiving and good God who gives me endless grace and love! Amen.

WISDOM FROM THE
BOOK OF PHILIPPIANS

*Be full of joy always because you belong
to the Lord. Again I say, be full of joy!*
PHILIPPIANS 4:4

Another book of the Bible to go to for encouragement is the book of Philippians. Paul wrote this letter to the church in the city of Philippi, and it's known as his letter of joy. The word *joy* is used over and over throughout the letter. The believers there had encouraged Paul and given him great joy, and he wanted to write to show them how much he appreciated them. He also wanted to remind them how real joy always depends on Jesus. As believers in Jesus, we can have joy even during times of suffering because we have faith and hope in Him to make us strong in the middle of it, help us through it, and rescue us from it. Paul said, "I can do all things because Christ gives me the strength" (Philippians 4:13). And we can say that too!

*Dear God, thank You for the book of Philippians.
Help me as I read it and keep coming back to it in
the future. Teach me what You want me to learn from
it to apply to my life and to share with others. Amen.*

WHEN YOU WANT REVENGE

Never pay back evil with more evil. Do things in such a way
that everyone can see you are honorable. Do all that you can
to live in peace with everyone. Dear friends, never take revenge.
Leave that to the righteous anger of God. For the Scriptures say,
"I will take revenge; I will pay them back," says the LORD.
ROMANS 12:17–19 NLT

Nothing is worse than having someone do something mean or unfair to you. Sadly, we know what that's like. Our instant reaction is to want to do something mean right back. If someone calls us nasty names, we want to call them nasty names too. If someone lies about us, we want to lie about them too. You know what I mean. But that's not wise because it's not what God's Word tells us to do. God wants us to let Him handle our mistreatment. He will do things with perfect justice in a way that we never could. Our job is never to pay back evil with evil but instead to live in a way that others see we are honorable and that we try to live at peace with everyone.

....

Dear God, it's so hard not to want to get revenge
on my own, but please help me to let You handle
it when someone treats me badly. Amen.

WISDOM FROM THE BOOK OF COLOSSIANS

Christ has brought you back to God by His death on the cross. In this way, Christ can bring you to God, holy and pure and without blame. This is for you if you keep the faith. You must not change from what you believe now. You must not leave the hope of the Good News you received.

COLOSSIANS 1:22–23

Paul wrote this letter to the church in the city of Colossae because he had heard that they were listening to false teaching that tried to add ideas from other religions to the Christian faith and the Good News of Jesus. Throughout our whole lives, we will hear about false teaching like this too, and so it's good for us to come back to read Colossians again and again to stay true to what God's Word wants us to know about Jesus and how to follow Him.

Dear God, thank You for the book of Colossians. Help me as I read it and keep coming back to it in the future. Teach me what You want me to learn from it to apply to my life and to share with others. Amen.

WISDOM WHILE YOU WAIT

Be gentle and be willing to wait for others.
COLOSSIANS 3:12

Waiting for things to happen or for God to answer prayer can feel like forever and can be so frustrating! Can you think of ways you hate to wait? But with wisdom, you can train yourself to have a good attitude about waiting. God uses those times to teach you to be patient and to depend on Him. Do you think it's fun to listen to someone whine and complain? Probably not. So you want to be careful you don't do that either while you're waiting. Let these scriptures fill your mind and give you wisdom about waiting when you're feeling impatient:

- "Wait for the Lord. Be strong. Let your heart be strong. Yes, wait for the Lord" (Psalm 27:14).

- "But they who wait upon the Lord will get new strength. They will rise up with wings like eagles. They will run and not get tired. They will walk and not become weak" (Isaiah 40:31).

- "The Lord is good to those who wait for Him, to the one who looks for Him" (Lamentations 3:25).

Dear God, it's not always easy, but please help me not to whine and complain but to have wisdom while I wait. Amen.

WISDOM WHEN YOU're really ANNOYED

*Most of all, have a true love for
each other. Love covers many sins.*
1 PETER 4:8

You probably know some kids who are hard to be around because of their annoying behavior. They get on everyone's nerves and just won't stop! In those situations, you need extra wisdom from God about how to be kind without encouraging obnoxious behavior. You shouldn't want to join in with other kids who might be mean to them or gossip behind their backs. Remember that every person, including yourself, can be annoying sometimes, and remember how much God loves each one of us! Ask God to help you interact well with difficult people and find ways to encourage them into better behavior.

*Dear God, please give me patience and peace when
I'm with difficult kids. Show me how to interact with
them with wisdom and grace and love. Amen.*

WISDOM FROM THE BOOKS OF 1 AND 2 THESSALONIANS

The Lord is faithful. He will give you strength and keep you safe from the devil. We have faith in the Lord for you. We believe you are doing and will keep on doing the things we told you. May the Lord lead your hearts into the love of God. May He help you as you wait for Christ.
2 THESSALONIANS 3:3–5

Paul wrote to the Christians in the city of Thessalonica to encourage them and teach them more about living for God and growing in their faith. He also encouraged them about hope in Jesus' return to gather all believers to be with Him forever in heaven. Then he wrote a second letter to clear up confusion about Jesus' return and to encourage the believers in Thessalonica to keep working while waiting on Jesus and not to get tired of doing what is right. As we wait for Jesus today, we also must keep doing the good work God has planned for us.

. . . .

Dear God, thank You for the books of 1 and 2 Thessalonians. Help me as I read them and keep coming back to them in the future. Teach me what You want me to learn from them to apply to my life and to share with others. Amen.

WISDOM FROM THOSE WHO HAVE LIVED A LONG TIME

*We. . .gain some wisdom from those
who have lived a long time.*
JOB 12:11–12 CEV

Who are the oldest relatives in your life—grandparents, great-grandparents, great-aunts and uncles, elderly friends? Do you enjoy talking to them? Maybe you have some great relationships with elderly people, or maybe it sometimes feels too hard to talk to and relate to them because you're young and they're not. But it's so wise to listen and learn from older folks. Think of them as the superstars of wisdom. The longer they have lived, it's likely the more wisdom they have gained from their many life experiences—and they can share that wisdom with you if you let them. Ask God to help you grow in relationship with wise elderly people. If you don't have any elderly relatives nearby, maybe you can start visiting a nursing home and make some new friends. Then let God teach you more wisdom through those new friends.

*Dear God, please help me to see how wonderful it
is to talk to elderly people and learn from them.
Teach me what You want me to know through
others who have lived a long time. Amen.*

WISDOM FROM THE BOOKS OF 1 AND 2 TIMOTHY

This letter is from Paul, a missionary of Jesus Christ. I am sent by God, the One Who saves, and by our Lord Jesus Christ Who is our hope. I write to you, Timothy. You are my son in the Christian faith. May God the Father and Jesus Christ our Lord give you His loving-favor and loving-kindness and peace.

1 TIMOTHY 1:1–2

In the books of 1 and 2 Timothy, Paul wrote to Timothy, a younger friend and pastor of a church in the city of Ephesus, to encourage him and teach him how to lead his church well, including instructions about how to care for widows (women whose husbands had died) and avoiding the love of money. Paul wrote another letter to Timothy sharing final words of encouragement and motivation that can encourage and motivate us in our faith today too!

Dear God, thank You for the books of 1 and 2 Timothy. Help me as I read them and keep coming back to them in the future. Teach me what You want me to learn from them to apply to my life and to share with others. Amen.

WISDOM ABOUT HEALING

*Jesus came to Peter's house. He saw Peter's wife's
mother in bed. . .very sick. He touched her hand and the
sickness left her. She got up and cared for Jesus. That
evening they brought to Jesus many people who had
demons in them. The demons were put out when Jesus
spoke to them. All the sick people were healed.*
MATTHEW 8:14–16

When Jesus was on earth, He showed that He truly was God
with His amazing power to heal people of sickness and demons. Jesus still has the power to heal now, and we can pray
and ask God for healing for people who need it. But we also
need wisdom about this. Sometimes God chooses not to heal
here on earth. We must remember that healing in heaven is
far better because it will last forever. So even more important
than praying for healing on earth is to pray that the people
who need it know Jesus as Savior so that they can be healed
in heaven forever with eternal life. As we do pray for healing,
we can do it with great faith, knowing that God is absolutely
able, but we must ask for it according to His will, knowing He
always, always does what is right and good.

*Dear God, You have the power to heal and perform any
miracle, including healing from any kind of sickness!
You are awesome, and I praise You! Please give me
wisdom as I pray for Your will to be done. Amen.*

WISDOM FROM THE BOOK OF TITUS

*In all things show them how to live by your life and
by right teaching. You should be wise in what you say.
Then the one who is against you will be ashamed and
will not be able to say anything bad about you.*

TITUS 2:7–8

Titus was a close friend and travel buddy to Paul, and Paul wrote the letter in the book of Titus to him to instruct him how to organize and lead the church and how to teach others to live for God. We can still learn much wisdom today from the lessons that were originally for Titus. When you act and talk the way God wants you to, others will learn by your good influence.

*Dear God, thank You for the book of Titus. Help me
as I read it and keep coming back to it in the future.
Teach me what You want me to learn from it to apply
to my life and to share with others. Amen.*

WISDOM ABOUT ANGELS

*"Be sure you do not hate one of these little children.
I tell you, they have angels who are always looking
into the face of My Father in heaven."*
MATTHEW 18:10

Maybe you hear people talk about guardian angels sometimes and wonder if they are real or not. This scripture in the Bible tells you that they are! Jesus said that little children have angels watching over them who are also standing with God, looking right at Him. So anything He tells them to do to help and protect you, they know it in an instant and can come to your rescue! Here are some more scriptures about angels:

- "The angel of the Lord stays close around those who fear Him, and He takes them out of trouble" (Psalm 34:7).

- "I tell you, it is the same way among the angels of God. If one sinner is sorry for his sins and turns from them, the angels are very happy" (Luke 15:10).

- "Keep on loving each other as Christian brothers. Do not forget to be kind to strangers and let them stay in your home. Some people have had angels in their homes without knowing it" (Hebrews 13:1–2).

*Dear God, thank You for the angels You have
assigned to protect and care for people! Amen.*

WISDOM FROM THE BOOK OF PHILEMON

Do not think of him any longer as a servant you own.
He is more than that to you. He is a much-loved
Christian brother to you and to me.
PHILEMON 16

The book of Philemon is all about a slave who robbed and then ran away from his owner Philemon. The runaway slave was named Onesimus, and he met Paul in Rome and became a Christian. So Paul decided to write to Philemon, asking him to please forgive Onesimus and view him not as a slave but as a fellow believer and brother in Jesus Christ. The book of Philemon teaches and reminds us to treat all people as equally loved and respected, especially believers in Jesus, because we are all family.

Dear God, thank You for the book of Philemon. Help me
as I read it and keep coming back to it in the future.
Teach me what You want me to learn from it to apply
to my life and to share with others. Amen.

WISDOM ABOUT HEAVEN

Then I saw a new heaven and a new earth. . . . I heard a
loud voice coming from heaven. It said, "See! God's home is
with men. He will live with them. They will be His people. God
Himself will be with them. He will be their God. God will take
away all their tears. There will be no more death or sorrow or
crying or pain. All the old things have passed away." Then the
One sitting on the throne said, "See! I am making all things new."
REVELATION 21:1, 3–5

It's fun to dream about what heaven might be like, but we also
always need to remember with wisdom that nobody here on
earth knows a whole lot about it yet. The Bible doesn't tell lots
of detail about heaven, probably because our minds couldn't
fully understand how awesome it will be (1 Corinthians 2:9)!
But it does tell us everything will be new and there will be no
more death or sorrow or crying or pain. That fact alone shows
us how awesome it will be!

Dear God, how amazing it will be when You make Your
home with us in the new heaven and earth You have
planned. Until then, please keep me close to You as I
do the good things You have for me in this life. Amen.

WISDOM FROM THE
BOOK OF HEBREWS

God made all things. He made all things for Himself.
It was right for God to make Jesus a perfect Leader
by having Him suffer for men's sins. In this way, He is
bringing many men to share His shining-greatness.
Jesus makes men holy. He takes away their sins.
HEBREWS 2:10–11

In the book of Hebrews, the writer (and no one seems to be sure who that writer is, exactly) wanted to teach the Jewish people who had become Christians not to go back to the same type of religion that was practiced in the Old Testament. The book's main point is that Jesus is above and beyond any kind of religious ritual and sacrifice. He paid for sin once for all people when He died on the cross—and then rose again! We can't make ourselves holy through any kind of religious practice, but we can let Jesus make us holy by accepting Him as the one true Savior who died for our sins.

Dear God, thank You for the book of Hebrews. Help me
as I read it and keep coming back to it in the future.
Teach me what You want me to learn from it to apply
to my life and to share with others. Amen.

Jesus' Wisdom About Forgiveness

*"Lord, how many times may my brother sin against me and
I forgive him, up to seven times?" Jesus said to [Peter],
"I tell you, not seven times but seventy times seven!"*
Matthew 18:21–22

Jesus taught us wisdom in a parable about how important forgiveness is:

"One of the servants. . .owed [the king] very much
money. . . . The servant got down on his face. . .He
said, 'Give me time, and I will pay you all the money.'
Then the king took pity. . . . He told him he did not
have to pay the money back. But that servant went
out and found one of the other servants who owed
him very little money. He. . .said, 'Pay me the money
you owe me!' The other servant. . .said, 'Give me
time, and I will pay you all the money.' . . . He had him
put in prison until he could pay the money. . . .
Then the king called for the first one. He said, '. . .I
forgave you. . . . Should you not have had pity on the
other servant, even as I had pity on you?' The king. . .
handed him over to men who would. . .hurt him until
he paid all the money he owed. So will My Father in
heaven do to you, if each one of you does not forgive
his brother from his heart." (Matthew 18:24–35)

*Dear Jesus, help me to forgive others
because You love and forgive me. Amen.*

WISDOM FROM THE BOOK OF JAMES

*Obey the Word of God. If you hear only and do not act,
you are only fooling yourself. Anyone who hears the
Word of God and does not obey is like a man looking at
his face in a mirror. After he sees himself and goes away,
he forgets what he looks like. But the one who keeps
looking into God's perfect Law and does not forget
it will do what it says and be happy as he does it.*

JAMES 1:22–25

The writer of this letter was the brother of Jesus and a leader of the church in Jerusalem. If you've heard and understand the saying "Actions speak louder than words," then you know the main point James wanted to make. Christians shouldn't just say we have faith. Our lives and actions should show it by what we do. That never means our good deeds are what save us from sin. It just means that when we have committed our lives to Jesus and we have the Holy Spirit living in us, we shouldn't simply want to listen to the Word of God, we should want to *do* what it says.

*Dear God, thank You for the book of James. Help me
as I read it and keep coming back to it in the future.
Teach me what You want me to learn from it to
apply to my life and to share with others. Amen.*

Be a Peacemaker, Part 1

Do all that you can to live in
peace with everyone.
ROMANS 12:18 NLT

Are you always at peace with your family and friends? Probably not. Any relationship is going to have some conflict sometimes, and that's okay if you do it wisely! Kicking-and-screaming kind of conflict is not good, but conflict with wisdom can be really good to work out problems—and we truly need it sometimes. But we shouldn't want to *stay* in conflict; we should work through it until there is peace again. James 4:1 says, "What starts wars and fights among you? Is it not because you want many things and are fighting to have them?" This shows us that so many of our conflicts are caused by selfishness, and when we are willing to work to make peace, we should be willing to admit our own selfishness and mistakes even as we point out selfishness and mistakes in others.

....

Dear God, please give me wisdom and show
me how You want me to do my best to work
to live in peace with everyone. Amen.

Be a Peacemaker, Part 2

"God blesses those who work for peace,
for they will be called the children of God."
MATTHEW 5:9 NLT

Other verses in the Bible, like the following, tell us to work at peace with others.

- "Work at living in peace with everyone, and work at living a holy life, for those who are not holy will not see the Lord" (Hebrews 12:14 NLT).

- "Turn away from what is sinful. Do what is good. Look for peace and go after it" (1 Peter 3:11).

When we look at how important it is to God to live in peace with others, it makes us realize how much we need His help with this. We need to keep asking God for His wisdom to know when to have conflict and when to let things go, and on how to show His kind of love and forgiveness to others through it all.

....

Dear God, please help me to value peace like You
do and to have wisdom to work out conflict well
with others when I need to. Help me also to
love and forgive like You do. Amen.

Be a Peacemaker, Part 3

*Let the peace of Christ have
power over your hearts.*
COLOSSIANS 3:15

If you want to work toward peace with others, you always need to be working on peace inside yourself first. Philippians 4:4–7 helps you know how. It says, "Be full of joy always because you belong to the Lord. Again I say, be full of joy! Let all people see how gentle you are. The Lord is coming again soon. Do not worry. Learn to pray about everything. Give thanks to God as you ask Him for what you need. The peace of God is much greater than the human mind can understand. This peace will keep your hearts and minds through Christ Jesus." And Psalm 119:165 (NLT) helps you know how to keep God's peace inside too when it says, "Those who love your instructions have great peace and do not stumble."

So, to sum it up—be full of joy because you belong to Jesus; don't worry but instead pray to God about everything; and love God's Word and obey it. That's how you can be full of God's amazing peace and then hopefully let that amazing peace overflow from you and around to others.

. . . .

Dear God, I love You and trust You and want to know and obey Your Word. Please fill me up with Your amazing peace every day and help me share it with others. Amen.

WISDOM FROM THE BOOKS OF 1 aND 2 PeTer

You are being kept by the power of God because you put your trust in Him and you will be saved from the punishment of sin at the end of the world.
1 PETER 1:5

Peter wrote 1 Peter to Christians all over the Roman Empire who were suffering in awful ways for believing in Jesus. He wanted to encourage believers and also teach them that suffering could be considered a good thing. That may sound odd, but he said, "Be happy that you are able to share some of the suffering of Christ. When His shining-greatness is shown, you will be filled with much joy. If men speak bad of you because you are a Christian, you will be happy because the Spirit of shining-greatness and of God is in you" (1 Peter 4:13–14). And in 2 Peter, written about three years after 1 Peter, Peter wanted to encourage Christians to keep growing in faith and warn them not to listen to false teachers.

Dear God, thank You for the books of 1 and 2 Peter. Help me as I read them and keep coming back to them in the future. Teach me what You want me to learn from them to apply to my life and to share with others. Amen.

WISDOM ABOUT JESUS' RETURN

*We are to be looking for the great hope and the coming
of our great God and the One Who saves, Christ Jesus.
He gave Himself for us. He did this by buying us with His
blood and making us free from all sin. He gave Himself
so His people could be clean and want to do good.*
TITUS 2:13–14

We should always be watching for Jesus to return because He promised He will! The idea of Jesus returning might sound a little scary because it will be unlike anything any person has ever experienced, but for those who love and trust Him, His return will be wonderful. Mark 13:24–27 says, "After those days of much trouble and pain and sorrow are over, the sun will get dark. The moon will not give light. The stars will fall from the sky. The powers in the heavens will be shaken. Then they will see the Son of Man coming in the clouds with great power and shining-greatness. He will send His angels. They will gather together God's people from the four winds. They will come from one end of the earth to the other end of heaven."

....

*Dear Jesus, I'm watching and waiting for You
to return and gather Your people, including me!
I love You and trust You! Amen.*

REAL WISDOM FROM GOD,
PART 1

If you have jealousy in your heart and fight to have many things, do not be proud of it. Do not lie against the truth. This is not the kind of wisdom that comes from God. But this wisdom comes from the world and from that which is not Christian and from the devil. . . . The wisdom that comes from heaven is first of all pure. Then it gives peace. It is gentle and willing to obey. It is full of loving-kindness and of doing good. It has no doubts and does not pretend to be something it is not. Those who plant seeds of peace will gather what is right and good.
JAMES 3:14–15, 17–18

This scripture in James 3 helps us know what real wisdom from God looks like in our lives. It's very different from wisdom from the world. In fact, 1 Corinthians 3:19 says, "The wisdom of this world is foolish to God." So it's important for us always to be praying to know the difference between the world's kind of wisdom and God's real wisdom. And we can only do that by constantly learning from God's Word and asking Him to show us how to use it in our lives through the power of the Holy Spirit who lives in us if we have committed our lives to Jesus as our Lord and Savior.

Dear God, please keep giving me Your real wisdom and help me see the big difference from the world's wisdom. Amen.

Real Wisdom from God, Part 2

What we preach is God's wisdom. . . . God planned for us to have this honor before the world began. None of the world leaders understood this wisdom. If they had, they would not have put Christ up on a cross to die. . . . The Holy Writings say, "No eye has ever seen or no ear has ever heard or no mind has ever thought of the wonderful things God has made ready for those who love Him." God has shown these things to us through His Holy Spirit. It is the Holy Spirit Who looks into all things, even the secrets of God, and shows them to us. Who can know the things about a man, except a man's own spirit that is in him? It is the same with God. . . . God has given us His Holy Spirit that we may know about the things given to us by Him.
1 CORINTHIANS 2:7–12

⁂

This scripture helps us to know more about the difference between the world's wisdom and God's wisdom. The key is the Holy Spirit, whom God has given us to show us the secrets of God. How super cool is that to be trusted to know the secrets of God? Keep on asking Him to share them with you!

....

Dear God, You are the awesome Creator of all, King of all kings, and Lord of all lords, and You want to share Your secrets with me. That's incredible! Please keep giving me Your wisdom through Your Holy Spirit. Amen.

WISDOM FROM THE BOOKS OF 1, 2, 3 JOHN

I am not writing to you about a new Law but an old one we have had from the beginning. Love means that we should live by obeying His Word. From the beginning He has said in His Word that our hearts should be full of love.

2 JOHN 5–6

Even though these three letters don't mention their writer, most believe it was the apostle John, who was one of the twelve original disciples of Jesus. When writing the first of these letters, John wanted to make sure the Christians then and now would know that Jesus was a real man and that He was also really God and that He loves us very much. Since John knew Jesus so personally, as one of His disciples, we can trust him. The second letter is a very short one to warn against false teachers. And 3 John is another short letter to John's friend Gaius to encourage him always to do what is good and not evil.

Dear God, thank You for the books of 1, 2, and 3 John. Help me as I read them and keep coming back to them in the future. Teach me what You want me to learn from them to apply to my life and to share with others. Amen.

WISDOM ABOUT FAKE GODS

*Our God is in the heavens. He does whatever He wants
to do. Their gods are silver and gold, the work of human
hands. They have mouths but they cannot speak. They have
eyes but they cannot see. They have ears but they cannot
hear. They have noses but they cannot smell. They have hands
but they cannot feel. They have feet but they cannot walk.
They cannot make a sound come out of their mouths. Those
who make them and trust them will be like them.*

PSALM 115:3–8

This scripture compares our one true God with the fake gods of
the world that some people make for themselves. It describes
how silly those fake gods are, with useless mouths, eyes, ears,
noses, hands, and feet. But people often make fake gods because they don't really want to serve or worship anyone but
themselves. And so they will end up as useless and meaningless
as those fake gods. But to trust and worship and obey the one
true God alone is to live the life you were created for, with
love, hope, and peace forever.

*Dear God, I'm so thankful I trust in You and not a fake god.
Please keep giving me Your wisdom. Help me to live for
You and do the good things You created me for. Amen.*

WISDOM FROM THE
BOOK OF JUDE

*Dear friends, I have been trying to write to you about
what God did for us when He saved us from the punishment
of sin. Now I must write to you and tell you to fight hard for
the faith which was once and for all given to the holy people
of God. Some sinful men have come into your church without
anyone knowing it. They are living in sin and they speak of the
loving-favor of God to cover up their sins. They have turned
against our only Leader and Lord, Jesus Christ. Long ago it
was written that these people would die in their sins.*
JUDE 3–4

There must have been a lot of false teachers in ancient times,
because Jude is another letter written to Jewish Christians
mostly to warn them not to listen to false teaching from those
who try to cover up their sin. God knew that we would need
this warning again in the future—again and again and again—
because sadly there are all kinds of people who want to spread
false teaching and try to hide their sin. We should always pray
for wisdom to choose right from wrong and to recognize false
teachers and covered-up sin.

*Dear God, thank You for the book of Jude. Help me
as I read it and keep coming back to it in the future.
Teach me what You want me to learn from it to
apply to my life and to share with others. Amen.*

WISDOM ABOUT
GOD'S GREAT POWER

[The disciples] took Jesus with them in a boat. . . . A bad wind storm came up. The waves were coming over the side of the boat. It was filling up with water. Jesus was in the back part of the boat sleeping on a pillow. They woke Him up, crying out, "Teacher, do You not care that we are about to die?" He got up and spoke sharp words to the wind. He said to the sea, "Be quiet! Be still." At once the wind stopped blowing. There were no more waves. He said to His followers, "Why are you so full of fear? Do you not have faith?" They were very much afraid and said to each other, "Who is this? Even the wind and waves obey Him!"
MARK 4:36–41

A girl of wisdom always needs to remember how powerful God is. Let this story in the Bible remind you that Jesus was able to command anything in all creation to obey Him. He could simply speak words to a storm to make it stop. He has great power over everything in your life today too, and He loves and cares for you. Remembering that should fill you with courage and peace to face any hard thing.

Dear God, I'm thankful for Your great power over everything! You can do anything at all to protect and help me. I feel so loved and safe because You take care of me. Amen.

STranGers anD aLIens

Dear friends, your real home is not here on earth.
You are strangers here. I ask you to keep away from all
the sinful desires of the flesh. These things fight to get hold
of your soul. When you are around people who do not know
God, be careful how you act. Even if they talk against you
as wrong-doers, in the end they will give thanks to God
for your good works when Christ comes again.

1 PETER 2:11–12

Some versions of this scripture describe Christians as being like aliens here on earth—not ones like you might see in a *Star Wars* or *Star Trek* movie, but aliens in the sense that we are strangers here in this world because it is not our real home. When we believe in Jesus as Savior, we know that He will give us eternal life someday in heaven, which *is* our real home. So we should be careful not to follow what the world says is wise and good and popular but to follow what God says is wise and good—which will often be unpopular in the world. That will help show others the difference of following Jesus, and hopefully they will want to follow Him too. Being a Christian in this world isn't always easy, but it is always totally worth it!

Dear God, help me to follow Your ways
and wisdom above all because I know my
real home is in heaven with You. Amen.

WISDOM FROM THE BOOK OF REVELATION

John tells that the Word of God is true. He tells of Jesus Christ and all that he saw and heard of Him. The man who reads this Book and listens to it being read and obeys what it says will be happy. For all these things will happen soon.
REVELATION 1:2–3

God sent an angel to John, one of Jesus' original twelve disciples, to give him visions to record. These visions were full of prophecy, imagery, and symbols of what will happen in the last days of this world. And all of that can often seem very confusing and sometimes even scary. But the main point of Revelation is that Jesus is coming soon to bring those of us who love and trust in Him into a new home to live peacefully and perfectly forever and ever.

Dear God, thank You for the book of Revelation. Help me as I read it and keep coming back to it in the future. Teach me what You want me to learn from it to apply to my life and to share with others. Amen.

WISDOM FOR THE FUTURE

"I tell you this: Do not worry about your life. Do not worry about what you are going to eat and drink. Do not worry about what you are going to wear. Is not life more important than food? Is not the body more important than clothes? Look at the birds in the sky. They do not plant seeds. They do not gather grain. They do not put grain into a building to keep. Yet your Father in heaven feeds them! Are you not more important than the birds?"
MATTHEW 6:25–26

Maybe sometimes you worry about the future, but Jesus promises that you never need to! He describes in Matthew 6 how the birds don't try to be prepared for the future, and God just feeds them and takes care of them. And you are so much more important to God and loved by Him than little birds are, so you can trust Him even more to take wonderful care of you! Don't ever forget this wisdom and let it wash your worries right out of your head!

Dear God, please help me to remember how You care for little birds so well and You love and care for me much more than them. Let this truth give me wisdom not to worry. Amen.

THE VALUE OF WISDOM

*Happy is the man who finds wisdom, and the man who gets
understanding. For it is better than getting silver and fine
gold. . . . Nothing you can wish for compares with her. Long
life is in her right hand. Riches and honor are in her left
hand. Her ways are pleasing, and all her paths are peace. . . .
The Lord built the earth by wisdom. He built the heavens by
understanding. By what He knows, the seas were broken up and
water falls from the sky. My son, do not allow them to leave your
eyes. Keep perfect wisdom and careful thinking. And they will be
life to your soul and a chain of beauty to your neck. Then you
will be safe as you walk on your way, and your foot will not trip.*
PROVERBS 3:13–17, 19–23

These verses in Proverbs are for all of us—girls and women
too!—to realize the great value of having God's wisdom. We
should never stop asking for it and appreciating it!

*Dear God, I don't want to forget how valuable Your wisdom is.
Please keep reminding me and giving it to me. Help me
to learn from and use it in everything I do. Amen.*

USE THE WORD OF GOD

Preach the Word of God. Preach it when it is
easy and people want to listen and when it is hard
and people do not want to listen. Preach it all the
time. Use the Word of God to show people they are
wrong. Use the Word of God to help them do right.

2 TIMOTHY 4:2

Not too many people like to be told they are wrong. Do you?
The Bible will correct us if we read and listen to it, because
it holds God's wisdom about what is right and what is wrong.
This scripture reminds us that we need to use God's Word to
show people when they are wrong and then help them do right
according to God's Word. We need to keep sharing God's
Word all the time, even when it's hard and people don't seem
to want to listen. And we can't share it well unless we are constantly learning from it too. It shows us what we do wrong and
need to correct in our own lives too.

Dear God, please give me wisdom and courage
to share Your Word and help people stop
doing wrong and instead do what is right—
and that goes for me too! Amen.

BUILD YOUR LIVES WITH WISDOM

"For I, the Lord, do not change. So you,
O children of Jacob, are not destroyed."
MALACHI 3:6

~~~~~

Everything in the world around us changes, sometimes quickly and sometimes over longer periods of time. Because of that, we need something that is always steady and stable on which to build our lives with wisdom. And the steadiest and most stable thing we can build on is God's Word. Jesus, who is "the same yesterday and today and forever" (Hebrews 13:8), described building on God's Word like someone building a house on rock rather than on sand: "Whoever hears these words of Mine and does them, will be like a wise man who built his house on rock. The rain came down. The water came up. The wind blew and hit the house. The house did not fall because it was built on rock. Whoever hears these words of Mine and does not do them, will be like a foolish man who built his house on sand. The rain came down. The water came up. The wind blew and hit the house. The house fell and broke apart" (Matthew 7:24–27).

....

Dear God, thank You for never changing and
for being my solid, stable Rock on whom
I can build my life with wisdom. Amen.

SCRIPTURE INDEX

OLD TESTAMENT